Real Deal:

Making Big Changes

with

Small Change

Real Deal:
Making Big Changes with Small Change

Marion Syversen, MBA

Norumbega**Financial**

Norumbega Financial

70 Main Road South
Hampden, ME 04444
NorumbegaFinancial.com

Printed in the United States of America

First Edition: October 2009

Library of Congress Control Number: 2009905458

Syversen, Marion
Real Deal: Making Big Changes with Small Change

ISBN-13: 978-0-9842546-0-6
ISBN-10:   0-9842546-0-9

Cover design by Luke LaBree / SutherlandWeston.com
Author photograph by David Brown / Northstar Photography

To the librarians of Hampden's Edythe Dyer Library, the best friends this book addict could have

Table of Contents

Acknowledgements

I've heard that writing a book is a solitary effort. Not so much in my case. The book before you would have been a big pile of mush, instead of the unbelievably clever tome you see before you, without the aide and assistance of some wonderful people. First of all, to my Book Club: Becky Ruggiero, Chantelle Haltizer and Chelsey Anderson each, and together, had a vision of what they hoped to see in this series. Vision, title, a series? All this, because of them. For little cash, a few fresh eggs and the occasional baguette of chocolate bread, these women proved to be the best of friends. How can I ever thank you?

Bethany Hunter, who was a kind and patient editor and, who with Chantelle and Chelsey, came up with the book's title, I thank you. Therese Madden, who knows me so well, and willingly dropped everything to organize and edit. Oh, my friend!

Sharon, Amy and Kathryn encouraged and read, and did whatever they could to help. To the buds who have listened, encouraged and cheered, and who even said, "I want to buy a copy!" I thank you. How lucky am I to have such friends?

And most of all, to my dearest Mort; it was good that you said yes! A lifetime's not long enough.

⮞ 1 ⮜

Finance
with
Chocolate Sauce™

Why did I write this book?

I love learning about money. I do! Not everyone does, of course. In fact, I've been around enough to know that many, many people find my passion well... shall we just say, unsavory?

Knowing this and talking to my friends and clients about it, I heard over and over again that while most people would be unlikely to request a book about money issues from Santa, people viewed money issues differently when I talked to them about it. You see, I've got great credentials... lots of experience, clients, education, even a spot on a local television show. But none of that has managed to change me into a traditional "suit," so to speak.

I understand what people need to know about living in a financially healthy way. I also know how to do it while living beautifully, which I define both as frugal and yet with a class and coziness that the un-schooled might otherwise have imagined requires deep pockets. More importantly, from listening to my clients and friends, I understand that most people need a friendly way to approach the subjects associated with the concept of living beautifully: both home improvement and financial

REAL DEAL
14   Making Big Changes with Small Change

stability. With all this in mind, I designed this book approaching these topics in a way that is fun and simultaneously useful and accessible. It addresses reader needs and priorities so that they are understood, utilized and – most importantly – so that readers will actually want to put wise counsel into active use.

That is precisely what this book, and the series that follows, does. They help you acquire essential knowledge about topics that many people don't exactly love. They do so by taking apparently bland subjects and using a figurative topping of chocolate sauce to make them not only palatable, but irresistible. And who can resist dessert?

As a young woman, desperate to learn about money management, I tried to figure out how to get control of our family's household finances. There were plenty of books to read on the topic. One author said, "Get a budget," but what we had didn't fit into the pie chart. For goodness sakes, the book said nothing whatsoever about how to deal with the fact that we already owed more than we made. How was I supposed to squeeze the big square peg of our debt and expenses into this pretty little round pie chart?

Another book said, "Pay off debt first," but we were using lawn furniture for our living room set and couldn't buy underwear for the kids. I appreciated the concept of fixing the mess that we had already made, but I knew that we had real, practical needs that we needed to address, priorities for creating a home for our family. I simply couldn't tell the kids, "We'll eat next year." While realistic in a purely financial sense, that style of money management wasn't going to work for us.

What I needed was a way to take control of our combined needs, addressing our responsibilities for over-spending in the past; the pressing concerns of our present spending needs, such as the lawn furniture; and the necessity of saving for our future. I needed a way to help me develop my inner tight-wad so that I could get control – serious control – of my, and our, spending. I needed to learn the value of money - how to save it, how to spend it, and maybe even how to earn it wisely - based on our life's priorities and the associated needs and goals.

Unfortunately, because the books didn't address my concerns, I didn't learn the lessons that I needed to at 30. Looking back, I made many mistakes, doing things that I'd never advise my clients to do now that I know much more. Since I am a financial advisor, I understand conservative advice and I respect its value. But my husband and I have taken risks that others might not have taken. We moved away from home, started businesses, had businesses fail, filed bankruptcy, and stepped in plenty of poo. We have been financially naïve and sometimes stupid.

I have written this book because you can learn from my mistakes. You can also learn from the wisdom I've gathered as I have learned to live beautifully and in a financially healthy way. My wisdom and expertise can help you address your financial past, present and future by teaching you how to seriously curb your spending. They can also teach you to plan in a way that will help you to realize your short term and long term goals. Many of you have also made financial mistakes and want to be responsible about fixing them. But you also want to live a pleasant present life, even while being stylishly Spartan in your spending. I will show you how to do that and give you the information that you need to plan for your future.

Eventually, my husband and I got wise, way wiser than we had been. I went to college and studied finance, getting a four-year degree, with highest honors, in only two years. I was inducted into the Honor Society and was Class President. I also earned an MBA, studying while working and raising my kids. I've run my own financial firm since 2001, helping all kinds of people understand various aspects of money and specializing in investments. I won the 2008 and 2009 award as Bangor's Best Financial Planning Firm.

All of this led to one simple understanding: there are only two basics about money: income and expenses. For most of us income is what we bring in through our job. How much do you earn? Can you earn more? Is it likely to increase? Will your income adjust with more education or experience, or perhaps if you specialize in your field?

The other side of the money equation is expenses. Spending less than you make brings stability and spending more than you make brings acid reflux.   Improving the way that you either make or spend can be enhanced by using a financial planning professional.

Keep in mind that all spending is an expense, even if your money is put into savings. Huh? Let me explain. When you save, you sock money away to spend in the future. So, saving for your Christmas Club, vacation, or a rainy day is an expense and counts as spending. Realistically, most of the time we are spending for stuff that we want to wear or sit on today, not for the future, which can be a problem, at least from a long-term planning perspective.

In our situation, I knew that if my husband and I couldn't drastically change our income, we had to address our spending. This book was born as we honed a frugal sense of style redoing our house on a veritable shoestring.

Why should you read this book?

I'm going to teach you how to spend very little money for household items, both large and small, as well as how to completely upgrade the interior and exterior of your house on the proverbial shoestring. If you use the savings to pay an extra $50 on the smallest amount of unsecured debt every month, you will be on your way to better financial health. Moreover, if after that bill is completely paid off you then use all the former payment + $50 to pay off the *next* bill and so on and so forth, you will be using basic pay-down-the-debt tenets to achieve financial health. Even better, if you also begin saving for retirement, you will be well on your way to financial Nirvana!

In other words, this book is designed to help you live in financial security, with an emphasis on "living." By spending a very small amount and using your noodle, you'll satisfy your yearning to make a lovely home for yourself and your family while getting seriously bitten by the frugal bug, which is a good thing!

Of course, it is important not to use this book as an excuse to spend money that you don't have or to get into debt. I have a lot of cool, cheap ideas to share with you about how to make your home lovely, but all of my advice is grounded in a strong underlying principle: Don't use the credit card to get there. Instead, squeeze money from areas where you currently spend to make changes a little at a time. You might think, "hey, I don't have even the smallest bit of extra right now," but with some creativity, you might be able to save gas and exercise fees by walking, soaking dried beans instead of buying canned ones, using tap water instead of drinking juice, or any number of other possible ways to cut a few dollars here and there. If you find just a few dollars in cost savings, you can use that money to buy a can of paint or fabric from the discount bin and advance your dream - or make an investment for your retirement.

You may be fortunate enough to have a larger budget for upgrades and changes; this book will help you use whatever amount you have in a way that maximizes the bang for your buck. Still, even if you are thinking of making progress with just a few dollars per month, the beauty that will be left in your wake will add up and you'll soon see the difference in essential aspects of the way that you live.

What's in this book?

I'm going to show you how we made changes without writing big checks for goods and services. Writing big checks would be spending 'Real Money.' Spending Real Money is buying things at full price because you're impatient or not as clever as those of us who do not do such things. There is only one reason to spend Real Money and that is for an item that truly represents a special treat, something that you have carefully considered that to you is worth the cost. From my point of view spending Real Money carefully is the only way to go, since most of us can't pay full price *all* the time or for everything. And why should we?

In order to begin to make changes, we'll have to get specific. It is one thing to talk in general terms about being frugal or making our home and garden beautiful, but I've learned through years of trial and error that the details are what count. To that end, this book will take you through the house, room by room, addressing specific ideas for improving every aspect of your home without spending much of your hard-earned money. I'll talk about storage, lighting, seating, appliances. I'll ask you to study pictures and take tours of homes and gardens. We'll brainstorm about using items to suit your needs and I'll be helping you to think a little out-of-the-box. I will also ask you to take your time and not rush these changes. According to research on the way the brain produces 'Aha' moments, you need time to mull things over and ideas on which to mull, if you will. "Insight does favor a prepared mind." (Hotz, 2009, p. A11)

Let's be realistic: when you save money, it usually means that you will spend more in time. However, like your financial budget, you can economize in ways related to time and thus make progress in fits and starts. Soon one room and then another will be transformed and friends will be asking you for tips and ideas. Yes, they will be asking YOU. This book will not only transform your home and your finances; it will transform you from a relative novice into a veritable expert on matters related to making your house beautiful and maintaining your finances in a healthy way.

How much time will each change take? That's hard to say, except that any change will almost always take more time than you think, especially at first, when you are less experienced and are probably doing things for the very first time. It will be very hard to even estimate how long you may need when you've never done a particular project before. Be patient with yourself. How would you speak to a child if he or she became frustrated while learning something new? Try talking to yourself nicely while you learn and grow, okay?

Mitigate some of the angst with planning. Have a spot set aside for the mess that may be present, such as the tools and material and miscellaneous bits and pieces. Move ahead with your vision. Unless your plans include vacationing in Europe while your crew redoes the house at your designer's direction, you will need to live with a bit of dust during a project.

I have to study things to figure them out. I do everything with an instruction manual, including household improvement tasks. Moreover, I was one of the craziest-dressing, uncreative persons among our particular set of friends and family. In other words, if I can bring style to our home and family, you can too. This book is the roadmap for you, my dear, to make it happen.

With my trusty honey by my side, I struggled in ways that you will avoid through this book. What? No trusty honey? No problem! You make the progress that *you* can make. You find the bargains that *you* can find. With a partner you may double the arms, legs and brains. But individually we are certainly up to any challenge! In my case, I would have made many of these improvements even if I had been on my own, though admittedly many would have taken longer. Also, because I lack expertise in areas that Mort excels, I couldn't have done all of it without him, and I couldn't have done it the exact same way. But this book explains how to assess your individual ability to make desired changes and aspires to help you figure out other ways to make the improvements you seek.

This book will show you what I've learned and researched about a variety of specific household improvement concepts. It addresses the science of color, which affects the look and mood of every room in your home, and the effect that different colors have on emotions. We'll tackle clutter, look at how it affects people and reveal some helpful ideas for corralling it with style.

And what about that lawn furniture I mentioned? I've got yard sale tips for finding great furniture and other deals and ideas for beautifying whatever you buy.

We'll get outdoors, too, and discuss plants and gardening and find creative ideas for your patch of grass. I'll share what I've learned about the amazing benefits of the great outdoors, which has enormous powers, from calming kids to easing road rage.

I'm going to show you ways that I have made decisions about where to spend Real Money, how I made choices about maximizing the few dollars that we had to work with. This book is a perfect example of frugality and choices, for costs were prioritized based on what I could scrimp and things that I felt were important. These priorities are individually chosen, meaning that what is vital to me may seem like a crazy expense to you.

The illustrations and photos in this book are in black and white. I don't love books with black and white pictures. But if I opted for color pictures in this book the costs would have been nearly triple. So to keep my costs reasonable, thus to make the purchase price reasonable, I opted for boring black and white pics. That said, in order to satisfy the need to see things in color, all of the photos will be available on my web site www.MarionSyversen.com. That way, we can make the book price accessible as well as satisfy our need to have pretty pictures to frame our discussion.

And like many things in life, this book was not only done on a budget, but on a schedule. Many Real Life interuptions and bumps in the road make up its life and story. If there are errors we will repair them in the next edition.

Future Planning

Spending Real Money isn't just about buying something. It is also about saving for the future using the least amount of dollars for the most effect. That's where early saving for retirement becomes part of this book. Many of you think it's boring, but I love this stuff and I can help you both to learn about it and to like it. If you are like many people and don't share my passion for talking about money, hiring a financial planner can be an important investment.

God bless him, my dear husband, Mort, thinks that I am hurting people when I explain economics and finances. He says that he can feel his brain getting hot and smoky—as if something is burning inside his head—when I speak to him about these topics. I know that my more enthusiastic approach to money matters is different from most, but I also understand the effect such topics have on people, regardless of approach.

If you feel overwhelmed by financial matters, you are not alone. If you'd rather think about something more fun, you have a lot of company. Many people feel confused; still more just find the topic boring. Lack of knowledge, understanding, or motivation is not a function of age or wealth. I have met people who have great wealth and multiple financial advisors, yet they still feel unsure about various aspects of investments, mutual funds and compounding interest. No matter what your financial status, if no one has helped you understand it, you probably won't accidentally learn things like this.

Financial services firms conduct studies to see how best to pleasantly give people the information they need to make wise investments. For example, ING, an international financial services company, conducted a study on the numbers people think of as important. In the study they asked open questions like, what number is the most important to you? How do you calculate the amount of money needed in retirement? They also peppered the survey with retirement planning info.

The study found that people may consider retirement planning (75%), but they generally don't like thinking about how much money they'll need in retirement (42%). Not surprising to me is that 39% of respondents think retirement planning is really boring. How do I know folks feel this way? Well, besides the fact that several good friends of mine absolutely hate the topic and my husband thinks – well, we *know* what he thinks… I'd say that half of my clients feel that exact same way.

It would be great if not wanting to think about a topic somehow made things not be relevant, but avoiding thinking about retirement doesn't change our need to plan for it. Is it any wonder that this study found that 80% of respondents would like the help of an advisor?

Learning about money doesn't have to be a punishment. This book will help you learn the information that you need to do this right. You are a responsible adult now and it's *your* money.

Don't put pressure on yourself, thinking that you have to know everything in great detail. For example, I don't understand computers; I just want them to work. I am fortunate that my wonderful husband likes the darn things and understands their every need. If I didn't have access to such a wonderful helper, I would have to engage a professional to help me—and yet I would still have to understand *enough* to be able to decide whether the professional was capable or a crook.

Similarly, you shouldn't beat yourself up about not understanding finance; you are certainly not alone if you are confused. But you do have to understand some things - like when to work with a financial advisor

- so that you don't find yourself selling apples downtown to make ends meet when your peers are enjoying their retirement.

Let's Do It

Mostly, when it comes to taking control of your life, including the finances, you must be willing to try. Be open to the possibility of success – or failure. Be open to not being great at something but only being adequate. Take a risk! You will probably find you have an aptitude for some things and stink at others, but what the heck? You will find gifts and talents that you didn't know you had and your new skills will develop with use.

I believe in you. You can handle this.

Grab my hand and follow me, little chickadee.

To sum up:

- If you find investments boring, you aren't the only one.
- Many people don't understand financial concepts, or charts and graphs, for that matter.
- Improvements around the house can be done without spending much money.
- You can live beautifully while recovering your financial health.
- You can live beautifully while remaining financially healthy.
- You can live beautifully while moving toward financial Nirvana.
- We will do this together.
- You can do it!

• •

✆ 2 ✆

How We Became Compulsive Fixer-Uppers

Mort and I began changing things around our house from early in our married lives. We bought our first house and the structure was sound and the lot was great but the living room was pink and contained art that didn't reflect our style. We changed the room with paint, then took out a second mortgage for renovations, and paid a lot more for additional changes. That seemed like the way you 'did' home improvement.

By now we'd been bitten by the improvement bug and wanted to make further changes, but we had run out of money to spend on professional help. That was when Mort got out the old chain saw and took out a wall and together we built – not very well, might I add - a bay window addition with a very deep window seat. In doing so we created a sun-filled office in what had been a mud room. We also put in a sliding glass door, replacing the old bottom-panel windowed-top door.

The work was challenging but not insurmountable and the added space and usable room was awesome for our needs. When we sold the house we found that the changes had translated into good value for the next owners as well.

Mort always believed that we should at least *try* the improvements that we wanted to make.

When we bought our next house, we overextended. Barely handling the mortgage, we pushed our budget to the breaking point, leaving no financial cushion for the changes we inevitably desired. Lacking financial resources, we relied instead on our own developing wherewithal. Whether it was a project that we had tackled before or not, we were gaining the confidence to know that we could figure things out. One time we started putting in a picture window discovering in the process a rotted sill, which we then ended up replacing. We constructed built-in shelving, relocating the kitchen, installed appliances, and more.

With nearly every project, we didn't do things as well as professionals. Or as quickly. It was our first time attempting many of these tasks. We read books and asked questions of the hardware folks. We drew pictures and took measurements and then eventually dove in. We sometimes had to do things again, but most of the time the job turned out at least okay on the first try.

Along the way we collected books on electrical work and carpentry. The process made us feel like, what the heck, let's try upholstery, or more detailed woodwork, or carpentry, or any number of "specialties." We invested in better tools to make the work more precise and less frustrating. We continued to covet the resources to hire folks to make the changes; we'd often wish that we could blink our eyes and have the changes be all done. I'm sure you understand. But we seem to be the type of people who envision changes and then need to make them happen, come heck or high water. We don't just sit. We have become two people who like to 'make progress.'

Through this adventure we have learned a lot; our knowledge is offered to you through the tips and information that is in this book. We've learned that reusing material not only saves money, but may allow you to actually get the darn project finished sooner because the resources will be readily available. Recycling can take more time and often is a pain, but the money saved helps to ensure that we get the room finished. We don't mind resting; weekends simply 'putzing' around would be pleasant. However, we also don't mind working, especially when the rewards make our lives better.

Along the way we learned that clutter is a pain. It gets dusty, needs to be moved, and gets in the way of progress, since to do many home improvement projects the 'stuff' needs be stored away. You may be surprised to find that it sometimes isn't missed when it's out of sight. Well, if it's not missed and it cost money, why have it? Time to recycle or call your favorite charity. Of course, sometimes folks hesitate to turn away from past foolishness and think that once they've bought it, they *must* keep it simply because they paid Real Money for it. No! Please don't pile new lunacy on to past lunacy. Instead, recycle where you can, have a garage sale and turn the things that you don't use and don't need into cash to invest in improvements that will enhance your life. Alternatively, give unused items away to the Salvation Army store, or Goodwill, or Habitat for Humanity, or any number of good causes that make sure that these items assist people in need.

I am sometimes asked where we got started. Honestly, projects, or ideas for projects usually begin with a frustrated snarl. "I can't stand how this room functions! I need a space to put these – fill in the blank: books, boots, computer, toys." Or, "I have no space to bake, slice, cook, cut, sit, put the mail, serve dinner, etc." Then the consideration of options began – remember, once you start, you gain confidence and have the power of no longer needing to live with frustration. Instead I think, I know that this is a good house, so what exactly is the problem? Where is the kink, the bottleneck? What's making me feel so darn cranky?

Once the question is posed, the real fun begins because it is then that I start using my imagination. In my dream world, what changes would I make? If I could do *anything* in this space, what would it be? Blow out the wall and add a room? This is a process of dreaming, brainstorming, thinking without limitations. It's free and it gets the snarl off my face, at least for a while, so I don't limit myself. I do start looking around for ideas. What do I like in my brother's place, or what do I think is cool about my neighbor's layout? Where have I seen this problem handled well? What do the endless catalogs that arrive in the mailbox show for solutions?

Now, comes the very important and clever bit: how can I make this change on a modest scale and for a lot less money than simply calling a contractor and getting out the checkbook? This is where the thinking and learning and mulling happens. I've learned to study the situation and become more clear about the options; this is the "meat" of this book and I will provide lots more information about how to assess and apply those options in the upcoming chapters.

Sometimes, I've found that I get stuck by the very scope of my vision, not knowing where to start. I've learned to start where I feel most stressed. However, there have been times where there is just too much going on in my life to tackle the thing that most makes me crazy. In those situations, I have learned to take a small piece of that thing and begin there. *Begin simply.* Pick a shelf and paint the back wall a different color than the surrounding area and rearrange the space. The paint cost very little and the changes took one weekend day. You have the time for that change and the budget, too. Or, get started with retirement planning by contacting a financial advisor. No commitment, just a first step. Similar options abound; I will give you ideas and suggestions in each section of this book.

Of course, I can't deny that it would be lovely if I had a pesky wand that spritzes fairy dust all around, making every project easy and perfect. No can do, buckaroo. But then, maybe that is actually a good thing, since we wouldn't derive any satisfaction from that.

Next Steps

Does eliminating the clutter really matter? Does making an orderly place *nicer* make a real difference? Heck, yeah. In upcoming chapters I will explain how and why it matters, then add more resources and suggestions as we think about the rooms in your house and the areas that we can change to get that snarl off your face. It isn't a magic wand, but these changes have a lot of power to help you make progress.

• •

∞ 3 ∞

Inside
My Cozy
House

Here we are! This book is about living well from every perspective, making your home a comfortable, warm, and cozy place for you, your family, and your friends while remaining within a stretched budget and working toward future financial security. We'll start with the inside of the house because that is where we do most of our living. In our case, I both live in my home and work from it, so making it beautiful and cozy has proved important for both my personal wellbeing and for the viability of my business. My clients come to my home (I have a designated office at the front of my house) and I want both my clients and my family to have an experience - aesthetically, emotionally, and psychologically – that helps them to feel cared for.

There is a compelling urge in many people, perhaps especially women, to make our surroundings beautiful, inviting and peaceful. It seems to be an innate part of our makeup to create a lovely environment for ourselves and our families.

As a structure, a house is designed with a far more simple mission, to keep people out of the elements. During a transitional time in our lives, when Mort and I were having trouble finding a rental, he said something that shows a big difference between how some men and some women see their house. Griping about the care with which I approached the search, Mort complained, "Me? I could live in a car. But you want a house!" I admit it. I want a house and he has since admitted that he wants something more than just a dry place to sleep, too.

As a nation, we watch home improvement shows, buy remodeling magazines and see pictures of ordinary rooms and houses transformed into

Without many indoor pictures, (Why didn't I realize earlier that I'd be writing a book?) I thought these dramatic before and after shots would whet your appetite. House has the old porch and ell (an ell is wing of a building off the main structure.)

beautiful sanctuaries. Unless you have had a custom home built to your specification, your home is probably not exactly how you may dream that it can be. Maybe you live in a ranch-style home or split-level and you yearn for the character of a colonial or the nooks and crannies of an older home. Or maybe you are the opposite: living amongst relics from the past and wanting to modernize.

In either case, we don't just dream of these changes. According to Remodeling Magazine we spend billions – billions! - of dollars a year transforming our houses into the homes of our dreams (Alfano, 2008, ¶ 3). Of course, if you have numerous resources, the journey from vision to reality can potentially be achieved with more ease. But those of us with a finite (read: limited, small, infinitesimal) amount of resources also have opportunities to live beautifully and well.

That said, maybe you have convinced yourself that dreaming is a waste of time because all you see are the obstacles. Even if you could imagine the possible changes that would bring your house to heights of beauty, when exactly might those changes be done? It's not as if you have a budget that is large enough to just hire a decorator to get the job done. Maybe someday you'll get the money saved to build the addition you want, but until then what are you supposed to do?

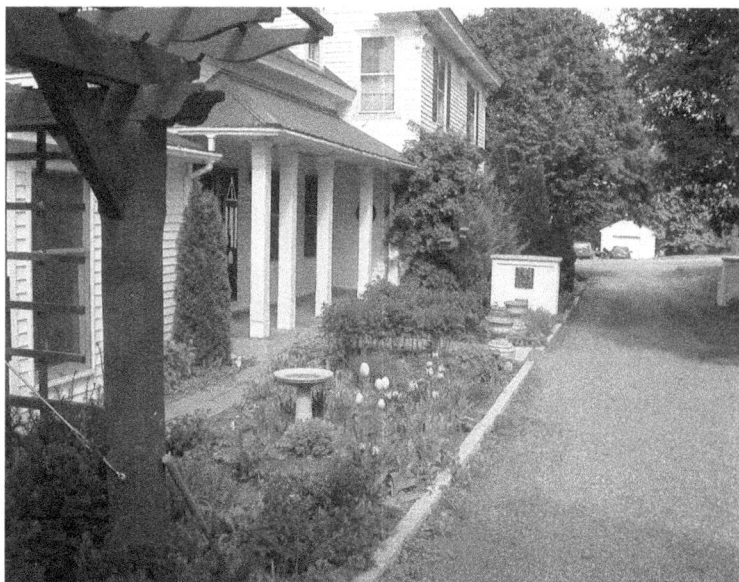

Family room addition and new porch with sheet metal roof. Easily available sheet metal roofing imitates standing rib metal roof, a beautiful but more significantly more costly product.

Just thinking about making changes can seem monumental. But what if you have toyed with the idea of making little changes yourself as a way to save money and want to 'just do it?'

That's when the next seeming obstacle rears its persistent little head: when on earth would you find the time to make even ONE change? There are so many responsibilities you're already juggling! (You're doing a beautiful job, by the way, with children that need your attention right now, dishes and kids' homework, the phone, the mail, a shower, the laundry—or even a job outside your home!)

Okay, take a cleansing breath. First, I know you can make changes, no matter what style of house you live in or what your budget. I know this with a certainty born from experience, my dear, because I've done it. As I plodded along making a few changes here, and a few more there, with my little, sometimes almost non-existent, budget, the changes added up and eventually the whole house was transformed.

I tried to wait until we had the budget to have a contractor come and completely redo the house and all the big and small changes in my mind. But when I grew tired of waiting I decided to try making just a bit of progress on my own. Oh, and I asked my husband for his help, too. We made changes bit by bit over time and the cumulative effect made an impact that made other people notice, admire, and want to emulate.

My friends began to notice the gradual changes I was making. When we would schedule a get-together they would say, "Hey, why don't we meet at your house. It's so much nicer than mine!" Acquaintances started asking for a tour – of MY house. A local reporter did an article on how my husband and I renovated our house cheaply.

What am I saying? With two kids, a husband, three dogs, volunteering in the community and all the other pressures families have, I started making little changes to my house. I felt that I had to do something and that if I was doomed to wait until some magical Right Time, I would never get to the home I envisioned. At this point in my process, I've created some rooms that make me feel safe and cozy and other rooms that make me feel as if I'm on vacation even when all I'm doing is slurping down my bowl of Cheerios. I not only improved my house, I improved my peace of mind!

In the book The Architecture of Happiness, author Alain de Botton listed the basics of design that bring happiness: order, balance and elegance (HGTV [Anne Krueger], n.d.). But much of design and happiness is personal; you may like being surrounded by your favorite items, like pictures and reminders of family and fun times, but others may prefer the simplicity of a clean, uncluttered space.

The importance of home as a place of solace in times of trouble is clear. Bad guys on the run from police go home. Where you live, your "nest," has a big impact on your psychology. Whether you rent or own, your home can provide comfort and renewal or it can be an additional source of stress for your already hectic life. I'm sure that you can think of experiences that reflect the serenity of a home, a place you visited and felt the tangible effect of order, balance and elegance on your feelings. Alternatively, we've all had experiences of walking into a house and wanting to leave right away, unaccountably distressed by the clutter or the poor design. Living well means developing the ability to individualize design so that the comfort you create matches your personality and the tone of the family life you desire.

Details

For example, as I mentioned above, I frequently eat my breakfast in a small room in my home that gets lots of morning sun. I turn on the gas fireplace and am surrounded with scrumptiousness: the warm, creamy yellow walls, the white seven-inch crown molding (made of multiple pieces of stock molding), luxurious drapes, chenille pillows and slip-covered furniture. The entire setting brings a contented smile to my face.

When I think about home improvements, I compare the feelings that I have about this much-favored room to the state of the room before we made the changes. Crammed with too much furniture and with no focal point, there was only one place to sit. The blue-green walls made the room feel cold, even with the morning sun, and the worn-out upholstery reminded me of the things that I wanted to change but never seemed to get the energy to actually accomplish. Swallowing breakfast wasn't very easy because all the places I looked reminded me of work I wanted to do.

By slowly making the changes that I wanted, I created a space that literally improved my life. When I experience that room, I feel happier, I am more productive at work, and I am a better person for my family, friends, and clients. It's important to see how much good you can do for yourself and your family when you transform your house, your tent, your shack from a location into a home. I know you can do this. You can change something about your house *this week*, without spending a lot of money. Those changes will change how you feel, and possibly even the harmony of your family, by affecting not only the beauty of your surroundings but the efficiency of the many and various tasks of everyone in your household.

The Relationship Between Home and Happiness

Do you find yourself silently wailing that if only you made more money, didn't have the pesky neighbor to content with, had a partner, and were truly appreciated at work, then you'd be happy? Guess again. These are external factors and research shows that happiness has little to do with jobs, money or stuff and much more to do with our choices and decisions. In an article in Allure magazine (Bailly, 2008), University of California psychology professor Sonja Lyubomirsky found that *we* control our moods through the thoughts, actions, and *attitudes that we choose for ourselves* daily. Lyubomirsky theorizes that since genes determine about 50 percent of our happiness, and 10 percent is determined by life circumstance, a very healthy 40 percent of our joy can be controlled through what we *do*, our *choices* and our *surroundings*.

This research creates a compelling reason for me to take my life firmly in hand and make the improvements to my life and my home that are needed to create the beauty I desire. If I dream of a more orderly kitchen, for example, one that functions as I think it should, with a place for backpacks and the kids' paraphernalia as well as an easy place to cook and clean in, I then want to begin making the changes. The action of doing something about the present disorder and the subsequent harmony of the transformed space is important both because it means that progress is being made and because the very process of acting toward that goal helps me to take control of and build a life that is happy.

Creating an atmosphere of order and beauty are what any home improvement efforts are about. By remodeling to reflect a sense of serenity, we do more than add storage, seating and comfort; rather, we build joyful family connections. If you are regularly correcting kids about putting things away, is that happening because there is no place to easily put their gear? Are you tripping over boots and backpacks? Maybe it's not entirely a sign of their irresponsibility or immaturity, but a sign of a design flaw, an inconvenient 'collection' method.

This effort isn't just about fulfilling an urge to paint and slipcover. It is not about action for the sake of action. Your family is probably already warm and dry wherever you live. It is about the positive influence that particular but simple changes can have when we make our house not just a place to sleep, but a lovelier place to live.

Train Your Eye to Beautify

Most of us are on budgets of one size or another. Even when we become convinced that we can and should redo chaotic, poorly functioning or dark and drab rooms, the process can seem totally overwhelming, from design and budget through completion. And how might we 'get the vision,' as my husband says, for these changes?

I have not always seen the possibilities in a house or yard, or even in people's finances. Maybe you already have a great eye for design. Me? I can't even dress myself without pictures of outfits that I might be able to duplicate with the separates in my wardrobe. I have had to really study pictures, design books and pay attention to TV shows to gather the ideas that I can use to change my surroundings. So, if you are not naturally gifted in this, fear not, because it can be learned.

As we discuss each room I will give suggestions that address the storage needs, uses, and extra touches that take the room to designer status while addressing the areas where costs spent show the best return. I will focus on inexpensive ways to make all of the suggested improvements. You can always spend more, but I think you will be pleased with the big effect the changes have and your friends will be shocked at the low costs of the upgrades.

After each project, as your confidence grows and you become just a bit more experienced, you will start to see things differently. You will ask yourself, "How can I use this new piece in the house or in this particular room? What interesting object will I find to use in this awkward space?" You start to find the solutions that you need as you keep your eyes open, working things out in your mind.

What's the best way to prepare? Be open to brainstorming and experimenting and be willing to take a chance! To begin to get the "vision" of what you'd like to see in your house, you need to get your brain filled with what you like. And remember, it may be just as important to figure out what you don't like!

Getting Started: The How-to's of Re-dos

Here's a description of inexpensive and readily available "textbooks" to help you hone, organize and eventually implement your vision. Of course, they carry nowhere near the price of actual books and yet provide an infinite supply of resources to support your visioning process.

Pictures

I began my remodeling education by regularly looking at pictures of houses and rooms that made me feel cozy. This is still one of my favorite ways to get ideas and to relax. I used to keep the magazines around to remind me of the pretty solutions to pesky dilemmas. But storage became an issue and I needed an easy method to find the one picture that I was looking for amongst all the issues. I eventually started a collection of torn-out pages of rooms or particular solutions that I liked.

As you absorb ideas for room layout, paint color or built-in storage solutions you will also be able to use pictures to get ideas for alternative furniture use. You might be able to use a yard-sale dresser as a kitchen island or bathroom vanity or even use a similar piece as extra storage in the dining room.

Creating this resource to fuel your vision has to be done, like everything else, with a tight budget in mind. Because magazines cost almost as much as paperback books, I was motivated to learn that you don't have to buy them to be able to read them: local libraries stock great design books and current magazines. Of course, you can't rip pages out of magazines that you borrow, but you could see if your recycling center or library offer older magazines at no cost. Your town's recycling center may also provide a drop-off for locals to pass on their books and magazines. Less organized sharing also works well: my friends and I circulate our magazines and rip out pictures we like as they pass from hand to hand.

In addition, there are lots of other free sources for design ideas. On-line magazines can be accessed from the convenience of your home; or, if you don't have a computer or access to the Internet, from your local library. Cable channels, like HGTV and the DIY Network, also ignite many ideas. Free magazines that also serve as catalogs are available from big box stores like Lowe's and Home Depot, which can also provide ideas and suggestions for various projects. You can also use traditional catalogs from companies such as Pottery Barn to get great pictures. Get as much inspiration as cheaply as possible so you can save money for the good stuff like paint and fixtures!

Use your digital recorder to record and print pictures from TV shows that feature an item or room idea that you'd like to imitate. If you don't have a recorder box, keep a note pad or paper handy so you can jot down ideas that you see, then make sure those notes get placed in a design folder or other location dedicated to holding your design ideas. In the event that you are likely to make particular remodeling changes years from now, taking notes will help to keep your vision alive. Then again, perhaps you are the type of person who will remember the great idea you spotted and maintain that inspiration without notes. Use whatever method works for *you*. The goal is to keep the pictures that inspire you the most so that you can dissect various characteristics from the ideal rooms to recreate a similar atmosphere in your house.

Making this house your home doesn't mean you should forget what home buyers generally like. Though I have no plans to sell my house, the resale value of my home is important and I keep it in mind when making changes that are more permanent. Remodeling with a potential, though unexpected, exit strategy is prudent and if and when you do sell, you won't have to make costly changes. Since I know that my tastes are consistent with the preferences of most people, I have kept my home's resale value in mind by paying attention to popular trends while also reflecting my own style.

File
Organize the pictures and ideas that you collect into files grouped by topics. I store magazine pictures and scribbled sheets of paper in file folders that we picked up for a dollar a box in a store's clearance sale. I organize my files, like this book, by rooms. I have files marked Living Room, Kitchen, Bedrooms, Attic, Bathrooms, Entry Way, etc. I've collected garden views and paint colors and pergola designs. I have saved some of these pictures for more than a decade because getting to the room or area outdoors just hasn't happened when I thought it might. Periodically I go through the files, winnowing out the older pictures as my tastes change or the file gets too big and bulky. Over time when the files have grown, I separate them into smaller categories: spare bedroom, master bedroom, kids' bedroom… you get the idea.

This filing system has become an invaluable resource for me as I improve our home. In fact, in many ways it provides the foundation for this book, so I'll get into the details regarding the content of my files in upcoming chapters.

Discover
Once you have organized your pictures, you'll begin to see patterns associated with the styles and colors that you choose over and over again. Similarities will emerge and become evident. You may find that you are drawn to rooms that are light and airy. I always seem to be drawn to living rooms that include paneled walls lined with books. As you study the details and examine what it is about the styles that draw you, you will notice how the fabrics, lighting and furnishings all work together to create the mood in each room.

Since this process is a mix of art and science, the implementation of your ideas may include some trial and error. I've painted some rooms in my house several times in as many months because things weren't working out the way I envisioned. The changing sunlight through the windows made the paint color seem too bright or too dull and the serenity I was hoping for just wasn't achieved. My husband will say, "You just painted this room. I think this color is fine, honey." But if I don't think it feels right, if I don't love it, I am willing to repaint until I am satisfied.

If you live in a house for many years, expect to update the décor. Most designs will stay approximately current for about ten years. For example, pay attention to colors that are favored in certain years, just to see the trends. Maybe you don't remember avocado appliances and tangerine wallpaper from the 1970's or the pastels of the 1980's, but the present color trends will eventually look just as dated as those styles do now. It really is amazing how much a thirty-dollar can of paint can transform and update a room. Frequently, a fresh color and a few updated accessories is all it takes to bring a room much closer to modern design styles—and you don't have to spend all the grocery money to make significant changes.

Try
Part of this whole renovation idea is you have to be willing to DO IT. You won't be experienced for a while, and you will only BECOME experienced when you do it a few times. My early projects were not done as proficiently as later efforts and in some things I will never achieve professional status. Don't you remember your first art project or bicycle ride or piano lesson? It wasn't great, was it? If you had given up because you couldn't do it perfectly the first time, where would you be now? Mort and I were willing to try this. More importantly, though we prefer excellence, we were willing to accept the possibility that we might not be really great at each task. Now that we have done tiling, painting and other jobs more than once, we've noticed a growing mastery. This will happen to you, too.

Getting Started Worksheet
I decided to paint a three-story house early in our marriage. I was excited to get the job started and see the changes! Mort burst my bubble with some wise advice, to start in the back of the house first. WHAT? He explained that this job was going to be big and by its end I would be in no mood to do the final details. The early energy I now had made that the best time to do the least favorite and least fulfilling job.

His advice was wise, even though it wasn't what I wanted to hear. There are two approaches you might take in deciding where to begin in your home renovation. First, if you are a more experienced painter, wallpaper applier, home improvement person, you've got the expertise to begin with the least favorite job. A friend who has a list of projects and re-ally, really wants to paint the Master Bedroom decided recently that making over the hand-me-down table before the holidays would be the tough job that she should do first. The bedroom painting is an easy task since the room is uncluttered, open and she has quite a bit of experience, but the table was less enjoyable and more onerous, yet as essential to the overall completion of the project. Instead of doing the fun and easy stuff first and then procrastinating about the other job, she got the less desirable task done first and used the paint job as a reward for getting the table redone.

However, if you are very hesitant or inexperienced, you may need to begin in an easier room, tackle only part of a room, or just a closet. In that case, doing smaller and less complicated jobs will give you satisfac-tion and will build confidence. The point is that you need to understand your own psychology and personality when deciding how to approach a project, using past success in any realm as the best indicator for how you get things done.

Planning Worksheet
- What furniture pieces do you think are important before you can begin the remodel?

- Where is your collection or file of pictures, paint chips and other inspirational items?

- Have you de-cluttered this space?

- Where will you store items as you paint, refinish, or update them? Consider an entirely different area of the house or ga-rage to store items that you find at a great price that fit your criteria for eventual changes in a particular room of the house.

- What are the storage needs of this space? This is important because lack of appropriate storage will create clutter. Let the clutter that regularly accumulates in the space guide you in addressing the room's storage needs, including shoes, backpacks, mail, etc.

Some Final Notes

This is new in some way to everyone, so be proud of yourself for each bit of progress you make. Pay attention to positive comments from family members on the improvements.

Enhance your ability to focus on the elements that you most love by having a yard sale or taking excess items (clutter) to a donation facility. If you have a yard sale, set aside money that you earn for yard sale shopping of your own in the search of missing pieces to redo the house.

Sign up for a class and learn a home improvement skill such as tiling, carpentry or upholstery. This will enhance your confidence in one particular area, which will then feed your overall growing belief that you have the capacity to tackle other areas related to home improvement.

Give yourself a gold star! You are ready to make improvements and get on the road toward living your life more beautifully!

• •

❧ **4** ❧

Color

I begin this section with a discussion about color because I begin my home improvements by considering color. It is fun to think about and it is really a core consideration when beginning to make your house a place to live beautifully. I love color. According to Design Basics (U.S. Army Corps of Engineers, 1997), color is the first thing people respond to when shown a design. I find that color is the element that is my initial determinant when I select art, plants or a handbag. I *need* it to feel happy. Author Oliver Sacks affirms that this need is a basic human trait. In his book, "*An Anthropologist on Mars*," he relates interesting and yet heartbreaking stories of individuals who lose their ability to see color, writing of the sense of loss, sadness and even suicidal depression that results.

Color Creates Energy For Your Home

Color is comprised of various wavelengths absorbed and reflected and then read by our bodies, not just our eyes. Light reflects color because of wavelengths. Some people refer to the science of reflected color using the general term "energy." Colors of the rainbow are distinct because of the wavelengths of each color. Practitioners of color Feng Shui use the knowledge that color affects people differently to design rooms of various intensities. Mood can be influenced by color, so having a basic understanding of color and its effect is essential.

Liking, or not liking, a color is subjective. But the reaction that people have to a particular color can still be accurately anticipated. Color symbolism involves the associations, based on historic connections, that people make between certain colors and a particular person, place, thing or event: for example, connections between purple and royalty, green and Ireland or red, white and blue and the American flag.

Writer C. Flynn had similar findings in her research about color. She wrote an article called "The Psychology of Colour" (Flynn, n.d., ¶ 6) in which she contends that there are many things that help us feel a certain response to color. These include memories, cultural associations, and even our own personality.

Understanding Color and Its Implications for Home Improvement

However, for design purposes, it is important to understand that our response to color is seldom a reaction to one color, but a reaction to a *combination* of colors (Colour Affects, n.d., ¶ 15). Angela Wright uses a grey sky as an example. If it's summer, the grey sky is a backdrop to the purple and pinks of flowers, birds flitting from leafy trees to emerald lawns or colorful boats bobbing on the water. This combination of colors with a grey sky is very different from the colors of a snowy winter scene. Both positive and negative emotions can be created based solely on colors and their intensities, and a balance of these tends to have a calming effect.

This balance can be achieved by using colors on opposite sides of the color wheel, which is a circle that shows the three *primary* colors and the colors that are created by mixing equal values of the primary colors together. (See the black and white illustration below.) You can get your own free Color Wheel by doing an online search. Graphics shops, web sites, paint stores, art supply stores, and craft shops all feature the color wheel along with detailed information about using color. Online auction sites such as eBay and others may also have color wheels.

The primary colors (P on the wheel) are Red, Blue and Yellow. They are primary colors because they cannot be created by mixing other colors together. Secondary colors (S) are created mixing an equally amount of two primary colors together. So Blue and Yellow make a new color: Green. Blue and Red equally mixed make Violet. When Red and Yellow are mixed in equal portions Orange is created, etc.

Primary colors are separated on the color wheel equidistant from each other and form a triangle. Secondary colors form another triangle. A third triangle is formed by another group of colors called Tertiary colors (T). These colors are a mix of a Secondary color and one Primary color. Red mixed with Orange form Red-Orange, Yellow mixed with Orange forms Yellow-Orange, etc.

Using the color wheel allows you to anticipate the vibrancy of mixing colors. Think about this: what is the reaction when opposite types of people get together? One might pep the other up. If similar people get together the level of excitement might be more subdued.

That's a way of understanding colors and their compatibility or energy levels. Complementary colors are opposite on the color wheel. A color scheme like this creates strong contrast. Yellow and Violet are complimentary colors, as are Green and Red, and Orange and Blue.

Monochrome color schemes use one color. There is no contrast and the scheme might be so soothing that it is monotonous. You would need to use different textures to create some interest in this scheme: shag rugs, shiny surfaces such as mirrors, and/or textured wall coverings and fabrics would help if you choose a monochrome color scheme.

Other color schemes are Split Complementary, in which secondary colors are chosen from opposite sides of the color wheel, such as Violet, Green, and Triadic, a combination that uses three colors equally spaced on the wheel.

Using colors that are side-by-side on the Color Wheel is called an Analogous pattern. This, too, lacks contrast but has more interest. In nature we see plants with analogous colors in the subtle variation of the greens and yellows in one flower's stem. Green, Yellow-Green and Yellow are analogous. I have made my bedroom analogous using violet, blues and greens. I think the room would give the feeling of coldness if left it with only those colors. So, I have used taupe, in the rug, and cinnamon brown, in the furniture, for warmth. Keep in mind that many colors can have a warm or cool version as you consider your options. Colors with a yellow – orange base are considered warm colors, while in general, blues, greens, and even reds with a blue base are cool colors, remembering the notion that colors may also have versions of warm and cool. Generally bold and energetic, warm colors get your attention while cool colors tend to calm.

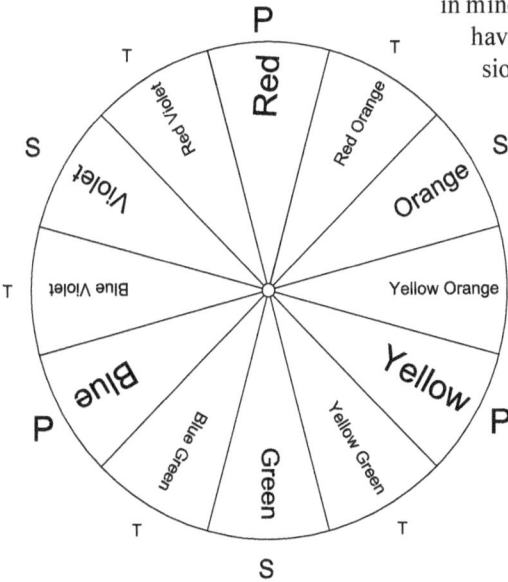

P = Primary Color
S = Secondary Color
T = Tertiary

Color Wheel

Warm colors are often used in rooms that do not receive warming light from the sun. My office's entrance hall is lit by only a small window on the second floor and the front door's window. The hall has a northern exposure, meaning that it could feel dark, even when well lit. I have painted this hall orange. It is not only makes the hall appear warmer, but it's got a punch of energy!

Cool colors are often used in rooms that receive plenty of light, or in which you are hoping for a calming effect. In my office, with many windows, I have painted the rooms blue. Large areas of the room are woodwork, and they are painted creamy white. Much of the furniture is cinnamon brown.

The Psychology of Basic Colors

According to Angela Wright (Younique Designs, n.d.), the psychology of eleven basic colors is as follows:

> *Red*
> This color is associated with strong emotions and is suggested as an accent color for this reason. Red raises blood pressure and increases appetite, but when used in small doses it brings energy to a room. Burgundy or pink should be chosen if you plan on painting an entire room in a red shade. I love red and carry red handbags a lot. The accents in my living room are dark red, like wine or burgundy. I also bought red paint for the back wall of our pantry's cabinets, though I haven't used it yet.

> *Blue*
> This color is universally liked and frequently cited as people's favorite color. It is mentally soothing, according to Wright, but can be cold. It can stimulate thought or calm the mind. Blue can lower blood pressure and suppresses appetite. (I like to use small, blue plates when I'm carefully counting calories!) In more than thirty years of marriage our bedrooms have always been shades of blue.

> *Yellow*
> The mildest of the warm colors, this color can be cheerful or conversely, can cause anxiety because it is an energy stimula-tor. Just the right tone is sometimes difficult to achieve and Wright encourages the use of a slightly paler shade than your favorite paint chip for best results. Our sitting room, which receives morning sun, is a creamy yellow. I use a taupe-y yellow in the living room on the walls above wood paneling and in complementary pillows and drapes.

Green

This cool color falls closest to the warm colors on the color wheel. People tend to experience green as restful because it requires the least amount of adjustment from our eyes. Green is used as the main color in Japanese gardens because of its soothing effect. We use blue-green in the living room and bedroom. Apple green is a favorite color of mine at Christmas and I have small accents of this color in other rooms.

Violet

With the shortest wavelength, purple, or violet, is enthusiastically appreciated by younger people. On the contrary, color research indicates that violet, or purple, is disliked by many adults, perhaps because of age-related changes to our eyes (Debbie Zimmer, The Rohm and Haas Paint Quality Institute, n.d., ¶ 7; (Yildirim, Akalin-Baskaya, & Hidayetoglu, 2006, ¶ 1). I like violet in the winter and apple green in the summer as accents for the bedroom.

Orange

Between Red and Yellow, Orange is experienced as the warmest color, but is less stimulating than red because of the addition of yellow. (DreamHomeDecorating.com, n.d., ¶ 3). As I mentioned above, a scrumptious orange is on the walls of the entry hall. When I had just painted it, it was so energizing it made me concerned that I'd jump out of my skin. Now that I have things on the walls and everything in place, it creates just the right amount of energy and warmth. Visitors frequently mention how much they like it.

Pink

Pink is a more soothing, less intense shade of red. According to Current Biology, when picking favorite colors females often choose pink or colors "that are a redder shade of blue" (Cell Press, August 20, 2007). I must admit that I have nothing in the house painted pink, though I love pink rosebud bedding and have it in the bedroom.

Grey
This color is neutral and, according to Wright, has no 'direct psychological properties." It can be dull if used alone. It can also be warm or cool. The downstairs bathroom is painted grey, with grey tiles. The sink cabinet is a pale maple and textured natural-colored grass paper covers one wall. The dove-grey bathroom walls make me feel soothed and quiet and the floor tile, which is a similar grey color that we laid in a herringbone pattern, ads some visual interest without busyness.

Black
Black is all colors absorbed and is an absence of light. It is a powerful accent color. Some designers believe that a room is not 'grounded' without touches of black to 'anchor' it. I use black accents in the living room and office, in things such as wrought iron chandeliers and lamp shades. Never would have considered black lampshades? Try them on chandelier bulbs or on sconces. It is a small touch that adds a bit of drama to set off the room's other colors.

White
A reflection of all colors, white can be glaring or can offset other colors to great effect. Museums use white as the backdrop for art. Some have decorated entire rooms in white because they work with color all day and they find visual rest in the simplicity. Some modern interpretations of country décor in major city spaces have featured rooms mostly done in white.

Brown
With a strong percentage of black, brown blends seriousness with warmth. Mixed with reds or blues it can feel soft or heavy. My pantry is a chocolate brown color. It was really hard not to lick the paintbrush while I was painting the room! It looked like melted chocolate and I kept imagining it would taste as good as it looked! The room, which is described in more detail in the Kitchen chapter, is quite small and lined with creamy white cabinets.

Turning Understanding into Practice

What does all this research have to do with you? Color is an inexpensive way to make a big statement in a room. Your first job is to determine how you want the room to *feel* before deciding on color. What *function* will you be performing in this room? Getting you or your family clean? Getting dirty dishes clean? Sleeping? Whatever the purpose, it is important to recognize that because this is your home, you will be doing more than an inconsequential task in that space; you will be living in it. As this book is about living well, it is important to consider carefully how color can enhance our homes and our lives.

For example, might 'getting clean' also entail more than just dashing from your pajamas to the shower to your daytime duds? Perhaps when you shower, you also spend time thinking about your day, using the time engaged in a routine task to organize your thoughts. If so, you may want to create a soothing atmosphere and consider which colors help you feel relaxed. A thirty-dollar can of paint can transform how you and your family feel in a particular space.

Further, as you consider the color of a room, it is helpful to think of the time of day that the room is most often used. Why? Because the color you choose will be somewhat different depending on whether it is lit by bright sunlight, fluorescent light or a few incandescent lamps scattered around the room. If you use a room only at night you might like it to feel cozy, so darker or more intense colors might help get that mood.

For example, I frequently use my sitting room on cold winter mornings. The sun's lower angle in the winter sky provides a very pleasant light in this room and I am drawn to it. To make the most of the happy feeling, I tried to create a space that would make me feel warm and cozy and blessed; I succeeded with this room and I get a smile on my face when I sit in it. The room is accented with white trim and for this, I actually had a piece of Wedgwood china – purchased at an auction- scanned by a paint-scanning machine to create the luscious creamy white effect that completes my morning coziness. I really *love* the creamy yellow on the walls. (Behr, 320A-3, Cornsilk.)

Practical Realities: Tips and Lessons Learned

Figuring out which color to paint a room can be quick and easy; for me, it rarely is, however, and I usually engage in much trial and error before settling on something that is perfect. My sitting room is one of the rooms that I painted three times until I was happy with the color effect. I had a sense that yellow would be perfect, but the first yellow I tried was too lemony. The next shade had too much orange for my vision. I finally settled on the perfect combination, but I learned an important tip that combines time-saving and economical advice: You don't have to keep painting the entire room if after painting a small space you realize that the color will not achieve what you want for the room. And while a partially painted wall is one solution, painting pros recommend that a sample board of the paint colors that you are considering would be even easier.

In my case, with this favorite room, I hadn't thought that I'd experience a problem so I didn't do sample sheets. I wanted a certain look and feel and was willing to continue until I got what I had in my mind. Believe me, by the time I was done I was very satisfied, but I was also pretty sick of moving furniture around and cleaning paint brushes. Ah, live and learn!

Your choice of a room color can get inspiration from many places. You might have a piece of furniture that you plan to use and its color or style reminds you of a particular color. The lack of sun or a view of the garden, or lake, may inspire you. I have even chosen a room color based on a particular piece of art. The composition of the piece is often not what I am first drawn to, but rather the colors the artist used.

Where do you begin the process of creating a color scheme that you love? It's easy, really. Dress yourself in an outfit that you love. Or look at flowers in a garden and examine the colors that you are drawn to. Take your time and look closely at what you've chosen and explore, think about, what it is that you love.

Let's use a hydrangea as an example of a flower with lovely color. A hydrangea is a mop-headed flower that blooms in mid or late summer. Varieties are white, pink and blue. Ah, but even in this apparently simple description, further observation reveals that we have only scratched the surface of the colors that are actually part of the flower's whole. A closer examination reveals that the flower is in fact several shades of these colors and bits of others such as green, taupe, brown, burgundy and violet.

Observing this flower's color detail provides an example of how colors work in home décor, working together in both obvious and subtle ways to create an overall effect. You could use the colors in this example to paint all the rooms on one level in your house; one room greenish-blue, one taupe, another green or burgundy. In this way you would be assured that the rooms would coordinate with each other and make the house a cohesive and calming retreat. Accent colors in each room could then be composed of alternative colors from the flower that were not used as the primary color on a particular room's walls. For example, the blue-green room could have a ticking stripe fabric in taupe and white, pillows in fabric with burgundy, navy and blue-green, and a sofa in a neutral microfiber.

As you begin to use your imagination, you'll have fun playing with different effects all while creating a lovely place in which to live and live well. As you play, allow yourself the freedom to take your time, as inspiration sometimes needs that time to really percolate into a full vision of loveliness.

As I mentioned previously, I have repainted rooms because the color didn't quite meet my expectations; it felt too cold, or too pink when I was trying for beige, whatever. I have read and seen TV shows that sometimes suggest painting large portions of a wall in the color(s) that you are considering so that – as compared to the tiny chips from the paint store – you can better get the sense which color would work better for your room. Try this if you like, or go ahead and paint the whole room—you can always change it later. Painting a room does not involve the thought and commitment of marriage, or the expense of a multi-year educational enterprise. Painting a room is a minimal expense and an afternoon's time. Stay calm. Do not hyperventilate. As a friend so aptly says, "There's not much commitment in a can of paint!"

Actual Paints and Other Necessary Tools

This isn't a decorating or a carpentry book, so be sure to consult an expert in the paint department of the store for your specific needs. In order to know what to ask, you should know that there are five basic finishes for interior paint: flat, eggshell, satin, semi-gloss and gloss. The finish reflects the level of sheen in the paint, with flat the least shiny and most matte of the finishes and gloss the most shiny. A paint's finish also indicates the ease with which you will have in cleaning fingerprints and smudges. Semi-gloss or gloss finishes are most often used on molding and woodwork because they resist dirt and wash clean.

When Mort and I paint a room, our personal preference is to use traditional flat or eggshell finish paints; we also generally use an inexpensive paint. With only adults living in the house now, we don't have heavy wearing wall coating needs. If you have little ones, a better quality paint will provide better and long lasting washability.

I often forget between painting jobs which finish of paint I use or need and need to ask each time I buy a new can. The paint store folks are very helpful and do not press unnecessary paint upgrade on unsuspecting shoppers. Don't feel shy about not being an expert and asking for help. You can't know everything and you don't have to. There are helpful folks at every store to guide you, but remember as you go in that it's not brain surgery, okay?

Different manufactures paints vary in their viscosity, or thickness, and I prefer a paint that isn't too watery. Mort sometimes prefers a different paint than do I. As an engineer who recommends various types of paints for industrial applications, he cares about the components of the paint. On the other hand, I care about the paint not dripping on my hair, so we have developed slightly different preferences. As you play with color and type, you will figure out the brand and level of quality that provides the right paint for *you*.

To get started, you'll also need brushes and rollers. Eventually, you may want to get a ladder and a wider variety of sizes and types of rollers and brushes. You don't need much to get started, but any job is easier to complete with a few good tools.

After you get these few basic supplies, you'll have everything you need. Better yet, many of the items will last for years of use if you make sure to keep your tools clean. Wash paint brushes immediately or wrap them in plastic to keep them wet until you are ready to wash them, but do it quickly. Dried paint on brushes is generally not removable and destroys the brush.

I paint with a roller and use disposable roller covers and paint trays liners so that I don't have to wash them out. I buy these items in multi-packs. When I use brushes for more detailed work, I use better quality brushes and I wash them promptly. We use old sheets or table cloths for dropcloths. I have 'painting clothes' that have *become* painting clothes because I have had a 'painting incident' on regular clothes. So now I have painting clothes.

If you've never painted a room, you might feel more confident with a few instructions. Written instructions and visual demonstrations can be found through online searches, at the library, or ask for free information at your local paint store.

Planning Worksheet:
- What room?
- What is the room's primary function?
- Its secondary function?
- Besides function, what feeling are you hoping to achieve?
- Is there an inspiration item for the room? (Art, fabric, etc.?)
- If possible attach a swatch to match colors.
- What time of day will this room most often be in use?
- Who is (are) the primary occupant(s)?
- What is her (his, their) favorite color?
- What is the exposure, or how much light does this room receive?

- Is lack of light or excessive sunlight important to the feeling you want to achieve in the room? (Rooms used primarily at night would not necessarily have this concern.)
- The room's primary color(s) will be …?
- Is this a warm or cool color?
- What is the trim or woodwork, molding color? (The trim does not need to be a different color than the wall.)
- Are large expanses of the room devoted to shelving, windows, or other things besides basic walls?
- What color are the cabinets or shelving?
- What view (color) is seen through the window(s)?
- Will there be window coverings?
- Will filtering light be important in the room's window coverings or is the purpose mostly cosmetic?
- If using window coverings, what color will they be? (They do not need to be a different color than wall or trim.)
- Flooring color?
- Ceiling color?
- What furnishings will be in the room?
- What colors are they?
- Where are all these colors on the color wheel?
- What is the room's color scheme? (Complimentary, Split-complimentary, Monochromatic, etc?)
- How does that scheme work with your vision for the feeling of the room? (Is it peaceful or energizing?)
- What primary color are the rooms that are adjacent to this room?
- If the adjacent room is visible from this room, how will neighboring room's color affect this room? (Are they complementary, etc?)

Frankly, I didn't specifically ask myself many of these questions, but I did keep a lot of these things in mind when considering the paint colors for all the rooms of my house. And since I got furniture after painting many of the rooms, I simply kept my major scheme in mind when I slipcovered or reupholstered each new addition.

We will use this color information throughout the rooms and outdoor spaces of our property. As you get started on your own home, you'll see what a difference this makes! Let's get inside the house with our next chapter.

• •

≈ 5 ≈

Kitchen - More
Than Just a Place
for Strappy Sandals

Some rooms in a house are more expensive to remodel than others. Kitchens are typically costly rooms to renovate because of the potential need for updated appliances, new cabinets, even reworked plumbing, electric or gas lines. Any of those items can add significant cost to a remodel.

Your kitchen may be the heart of your home, a place where you bake bread from scratch and cook up a storm on a regular basis. Alternatively, maybe you store your shoes in the oven and only pass through the kitchen when you're looking for your strappy sandals. For many of us the kitchen is the place where we make the kids' meals, share their secrets, finger paint, and build volcanoes. We huddle over a warm cup of cocoa on cold mornings and long nights.

But what if your space for such important tasks is dark and dirty, with appliances from the 1950's, broken drawer knobs and an oven that cooks unevenly? What if the flooring is peeling and the cabinets are held together with spare parts and prayer? The likelihood of developing any additional culinary skills or of spending anytime in a room that looks that scary is slight. You're probably making mortgage payments for this space. For the money, you should have a clean and efficient room. We should set our sights higher and aim for beauty, too.

Motivation

Kitchen renovations are the major factor in determining a home's resale value, according to Barbara Corcoran, real estate expert and author (HGTV []). However, in 2008 the average cost of a kitchen remodel was $15-$20 thousand dollars, which may make your vision for a modernized kitchen seem impossible. However, it starts to feel like a more viable option when we consider that 94%- 100% of remodeling costs will be recovered in the sale of your home if you spend no more than 20% of your home's value on the total kitchen renovation budget (Rona, n.d., ¶ 1). By implementing careful renovation ideas, you can spend less money and potentially add thousands of dollars in value to your home with hard work and imagination. Mort and I redid our kitchen for less than $4,000, a figure that included new, 'upgraded' appliances that we added after the original renovation.

But, really, $15- $20 thousand dollars? Why does it cost so much? Kitchen renovation can be expensive for several reasons. Labor is a major cost and typically comprises about 30% of the remodeling budget, according to experts (Estimate the Cost, ¶ 2). Plumbing and wiring are major elements in the kitchen and working with or relocating these elements can be dangerous if you don't know what you're doing. If your dream includes a total kitchen transformation, reconnoitering the floor plan so that the sink is moved to an opposite side of the room, or even putting the kitchen in another room of the house, it may be a good idea to hire a plumber to do that portion of the work. On the other hand, you might learn to do these jobs yourself by taking classes at community colleges or participating in workshops at the big box stores. Paying for professional help can be the best option in some cases, but you don't want to spend money if you don't have to. Check with building and electrical codes for your town; remember, safety first!

Considerations

Renovations take time, too, so consider your lifestyle as you make a decision about whether to do the labor yourself or hire some help. If you are already commuting many hours each day, you may not want to spend your weekends plumbing. In that case, spending money to have the work completed may save you time and give you peace of mind. That said, it is also possible that you might find the work so different from your regular job that it becomes a relaxing and satisfying task that you like to do because of the sense of accomplishment that it brings. If so, consider working with a buddy; find someone from church, a neighbor, or a coworker and partner with each other, helping to complete larger projects in each other's homes together. Kind of like the Hitchcock

Oh, baby, me in a mask! Had I known I'd be sharing 'before and after' images in a book, believe you me, I would have taken more than the very few pictures we took. Allergies and dust prompted my adornment with the attractive safety gear. 'Nuff said.

movie, 'Strangers on a Train,' but instead of getting a buddy to help you commit a murder, partner for home renovation!

Planning

Take time to think about what works in the kitchen and what doesn't. You may have waited so long that you are so tired of whatever is bugging you that you want to trash the whole space. Try to be objective, though. Can the cabinets, which may presently be plain or not a great color, be salvaged and used creatively in their present location or in another room? Can you use them back-to-back in the creation of an

From the kitchen island, looking into what is now the Pantry. You can also see the closet to the left of the double ovens that is another storage area and has the automatic lights turn on when the door opens.

island? Even if you have a big budget, grab a frugal friend and think the project through.

You might want to start by drawing out plans. Investigate computer design programs that make things three dimensional and provide standard measurements for cabinets, a sink, etc. If making exact floor plans works for you, then do it.

An important way to save money is to avoid certain actions. Do NOT radically relocate the plumbing and wiring. Keep the present floor plan of the kitchen; if you decide you must move the sink or stove, don't move it far. In the renovations of our home in Hampden, Maine, Mort and I chose not to move the kitchen sink, as we knew that this would affect plumbing in major and expensive ways. Instead, we achieved the overall efficiency that we sought by moving the stove from its original location, separating the unit into a cook top and oven, and then placing both in different places than they were in the original floor plan.

Beautify: What's In The File?

I have two files that have kitchen and kitchen storage ideas: Kitchen and Pantry. If you have plans for a Dining Room, because of their similar and complementary functions, they could be compiled together.

In the Kitchen file I have saved several articles on kitchen lighting design—it is dark in Maine during the winter months and you could hurt yourself if you don't have adequate lighting! I have a fabric swatch stapled to a magazine ad for a fancy range. (I kept this ad for the wall color pictured in it, not the stove.) I have pictures of islands and pretty benches, cabinets in colors that I might want to try, elaborate window covers, shiny silver trays and space-saving articles. I also have a list of sources for inexpensive glass for cabinet door inserts. The Pantry file has clever storage ideas for table linens, oversized plates, or trays and cans. Both of these files help me to think about what I want in a kitchen, providing insight about the overall design that most appealed to me as well as offering specific resources as I began to make that vision a reality.

How are cost-effective and inexpensive improvements created? With details and special objects. Through careful consideration and advance planning, you pay attention to the details that make a difference in a kitchen. By knowing what you really value and doing creative and diligent research about acquisition options, you can add special objects wisely, knowing when to splurge and when to find substitutes. You might splurge and buy the faucet you crave, affording this because in other areas, you scrimp and purchase the inexpensive ivory tiles, reuse and recycle, and/or get creative with crown molding, unusual handles and drawer pulls. Doing this allows you to be judicious about how you spend your money, knowing what you really value and when expense is merely convenient. If you have your heart set on a particular item and you want it to be exactly that item and no substitute, know that that is your splurge item and then save for it and really enjoy it!

Maximize

Our Hampden kitchen is not large. There are 17 linear feet of cabinets in the main kitchen area and they do not extend to the 8.5 foot ceilings. We could have used the space all the way to the ceiling, taking advantage of easy cabinet additional storage. However, as much as I value storage, I vetoed that option. Why? First, because the room would feel one foot *smaller* since that is the depth of a standard upper cabinet, and I wanted the room to feel larger. Additionally, I am short and am only barely able to reach the items

Corner Cabinet- Melamine corner cabinet unit made more custom with door cut out, glass inserted and simple molding covering the chipped up melamine from our inexperience with the saw blade. Colorful pitchers, vases and other knick knacks have a featured home in this space. In the ceramic plant pots is the kitchen's 'bling.'

on the upper shelves. Higher shelves would therefore not only crowd the feeling of the room, they would create a storage "solution" that just wouldn't work for our personal needs.

Still, 17 feet of cabinets is not much, not when my overall coziness requires storage to eliminate the feeling of clutter. Knowing this, we addressed that potential problem by adding an island and creating four more feet of drawer and cabinet storage under the cooktop. When deciding on the size of our island, we took into account both aesthetic and utilitarian considerations. Having made these decisions, Mort then made the island himself. This was done to absolutely maximize our dimensions without having to pay for a custom piece built by a carpenter, which we knew could be expensive. We didn't have a lot of experience in building cabinets before this project; in fact, Mort had never built so much as a drawer before. But we figured that we had to start somewhere and our earlier efforts with paint and other improvements had given us the confidence to know that we wouldn't risk much by trying. We bought plywood one piece at a time and then began to purchase drawer slides as we scraped together the money to do so.

Another popular storage idea that I love is to line a shallow wall with cabinets from floor to ceiling. Determine an upper and lower cabinet partition if you like and have narrower cabinets above and deeper cabinets below for a built-in hutch look. You could even add a counter to the lower cabinets and place the upper cabinets on that to provide a handy service or display area. We made a 'hutch in the pantry by stacking three recycled kitchen cabinets (the upper cabinets are one foot deep, lower cabinets are two feet deep, upper cabinets directly on top of each other) and then set a piece of Formica to make a transition to the final, and deeper lower cabinet underneath. This new unit adds nine essential feet of cabinet storage to the pantry. The remodeled cabinet fronts are now outfitted in glass and provide storage for the lovely estate sale china pieces, candle sticks, and pretty bowls we've acquired. The lower storage area, which is enclosed holds the dog's food and other less attractive items.

Use every nook and cranny. I suggest using furniture pieces that will maximize all the available space. Why use a storage piece like a typical side board, with open space on the lower portion and no storage capacity if storage space is needed? Instead, use a piece that allows storage from its top to the floor and then store to your heart's content. For example, we don't have an 'office' per se in the kitchen because we just don't have the space. However, bills, flyers, and other notes still end up in the kitchen, of course, because that is where our family gravitates. To address this, I've created a mix of storage solutions to hold post-its, the phone, notepads, etc.

I did it in a unique way that took advantage of the current design and décor in the room. Our phone sits atop an old record cabinet that is 39 inches tall, 19 inches wide and 15 inches deep. This is perfect for the very small space that we have. The two narrow cabinet doors hide adjustable shelves and we have them set up to hold phone books, bills, and restaurant take-away menus. The cabinet also holds my library books. Besides the phone, the top holds the cell phone battery charger so we can easily plug in our devices. Post-its and pens are neatly stored here, too. Hanging on the wall above this is the key rack and the dog's leash. And above the key rack is a small mirror that allows us to check our appearance as we dash out the door.

The cabinet does not go all the way to the floor, though very nearly. The 10 inches from the bottom of the unit to the floor was potentially wasted space that I knew I needed! I went to a container store and bought a faux leather box, 12 by 15.5 inches, which fits perfectly under the unit and tucks between the legs so it looks tidy. In that box I keep the many periodicals that I get in the mail every day until I've had a chance to read them. This entire unit is both a beautiful and a utilitarian solution to the problem common to many kitchens: keeping available counter space less cluttered with the daily mail that so quickly piles up.

It is important to maximize available space by finding creative ways to address recurring clutter dilemmas. Since our house was built in the 1800's when the practice was to enter from the front door of the house, our now regularly used kitchen area had no spot for coats. After surveying the kitchen one too many times and seeing coats hanging on every chair back, I snarled, then stepped back to try to figure out what could be done to solve what was obviously more of a storage problem than a behavior issue.

The solution was simple: a 14 inch wide coat-cubby that we placed next to the refrigerator. Cabinets make an "L" going to the left of the fridge, the new 'coat-cubby' is on the right. Four hooks hold just a few coats, but those are enough to keep the room free of coats - most of the time! The present kitchen cabinets are white melamine. A cabinet that I can barely reach is above the refrigerator, and if you are familiar with how some of those units are made, the cabinet has very long sides that encompass the fridge and serve as legs for the upper cabinet. Mort bought a sheet of white melamine, cut it into the pieces needed to attach to the segway from the refrigerator. The pieces are attached with 'L' brackets and at 74 inches tall the cubby has an upper shelf, in which I've placed a bracket that holds hats and gloves, and there is space at the bottom for my purse, as well as messy shoes or boots. On the outside of the coat-cubby, still farther to the right and near the telephone,

Coat Cubby- This simple unit has outside dimensions of slightly more than 14" which are specific to our house and the existing molding and door way which it abuts. When we use it, it works well!

we hung a bulletin board that holds a calendar and pictures and reminders. This isn't a huge space, but it holds just enough to keep the kitchen that much less cluttered.

To address such issues in your own home, it is often helpful to begin by looking up. Is there wall space that might hold attractive storage? Consider building shelves, perhaps using a closet organizer, the build-a-closet boxes with drawers that are available at large home improvement stores for shallow, inexpensive storage solutions. Stack them for more effect. Line a wall with them. They come in several colors and basic styles and will work in many rooms of your house.

Needed utility also comes with consideration of how space is used. To the left of our double oven we added a two foot closet that we had originally used as a broom closet. I noticed that when we both cooked we both needed to get into one small section of our renovated kitchen. I snarled, "What is up with this?" one too many times, then remembered to rephrase the question in improvement terms: "What can we do with our space to get us working in other spots?"

I spoke with Mort and we decided to move the vacuum and the brooms that we had stored in the existing closet to other less prime locations. We then decided to use that closet in a completely different way from its original intention and built shelves within the closet *and on the door.* Mort even added lights inside with a switch that automatically comes on when the door is open and turns off when the door is closed. Now we have a two foot wide, six foot tall closet to store food right where we need it. Better yet, after we first installed it, we had ready entertainment as I – just for fun – repeatedly opened and closed the door just to see the light go on and off and showed it to all of our friends!

Another way that we maximized was to look at a relatively minor issue, but one that I've noticed plagued many family chefs. I don't know about you, but drawer space for utensils wasn't adequate in our kitchen. This need led me to notice that cooks often store their frequently used, larger serving pieces on their counters, which facilitates the meal preparation process by having necessary tools readily available. Using the countertop for storing a few things – though not enough to violate my anti-clutter preference - can blend function and style.

I combined this utilitarian realization with my own design preferences by putting our long-handled cooking utensils in an attractive ceramic plant pot, which I store on the counter. Following that theme, I then sorted short-handled serving pieces in a more diminutive container, which I also set on the countertop. For this container, I admit that I yearned for an expensive, pretty jardinière from France, but instead I filled a $13 pot with a slew of shiny ladles and spatulas that I purchased in a box lot at an estate sale for $40. It looks gorgeous, adds a bit of 'bling' to the countertop and keeps my needed cooking gear within easy reach!

Getting Specific: Kitchen Cabinets

A big cost of kitchen renovations is the cabinets, which can represent as much as 40% of the total renovation budget (Kitchen Remodel Ideas, n.d., ¶ 1). Before you begin, consider: what is important to you about cabinets? Personally, I want cabinets that will easily wash clean inside and out. I don't care what the guts of the cabinets are made of so long as they are strong and washable. I do want beauty, but I only want it superficially. By this I mean that I don't need or want the expense of furniture-grade cabinets, though I do want them to look as grand as those in the kitchens in the magazines and those on the best home tours.

If you plan on improving your kitchen with store-bought cabinets, you can often get free design help from the team at the store. They will have ideas and will work with your vision to make viable plans. If you plan on reusing the existing cabinets, making cabinets yourself, buying off-the-shelf units, or finding suitable items from yard sales, then a design plan is especially important. Create it with the level of detail that works for you and your work buddy.

If your present cabinets are relatively modern wood cabinets, they can be painted or stained. This inexpensive change will modernize your room for little money. If you choose this route take the time for proper preparation or you will rue the day you took a shortcut. This will take different forms based on your existing cabinets and your desired outcome. Depending on the type of finish now on the cabinets and the changes you want to make, I suggest that you remove a door from one of the cabinets and bring it to an expert at a specialty paint store such as

Sherwin Williams. Let the experts tell you how to tackle the job. You will at least need to thoroughly clean the cabinets before painting but you may also need to seal them or sand them, and maybe even both. As your plans develop, consider all options. Make a change that is radical; go from light to dark or dark to light. Transform your mood with paint. Install new handles and knobs. Make new doors, cover them with textured wallpaper, add molding trim, or order new doors from a custom shop or a big box store. Have fun!

Mixing it up will make your kitchen look like it was custom-designed by a top interior professional. You'll notice as you begin your collection of files that magazines and design center displays sometimes feature several styles or colors of cabinets in one kitchen. The upper cabinets may be white and the lower ones red. The island cabinets may be stained a medium brown. Lately I've noticed all-white cabinets with island cabinets in black.

Other considerations have to do with shelving. You may opt for upper cabinets that have open shelving, or you may use glass doors on upper cabinets and closed storage below. I think for ease of cleaning, closed storage is the easiest and least time-consuming. The baskets hanging above the cooktop island, a-la the 1980s, were a cleaning nightmare for me! I much prefer the ease of satin-finish cabinet faces for quick cleaning.

Another option is to use cabinets on one wall that imitate a Welsh hutch, which is simply a very large open upper shelf that displays prettier dishes, bowls or platters, and a large, closed lower storage area. You might want to make this piece stand out, in which case you might consider painting it a different color than the rest of the kitchen cabinets. If you want to make the cabinetry on another wall look like a separate unit, paint it with an accent color. These kinds of details and custom touches do not cost much at all, but they are essential ideas to make your bargain kitchen *look* more expensive.

Paint isn't the only way to add detail. Perhaps the cabinets seem too plain and you'd prefer more detail? Add molding, in a simple or complex mix. Or add a rectangle of textured wallpaper and edge that with a border of molding. We added an upper, crown molding topping – which we bought at a yard sale- to our flat-fronted cabinets to make them look a bit more traditional.

We also added more storage to the kitchen, using the upper portion of a salvaged hutch that we got at the dump, FOR FREE. The doors of the unit are now frosted glass and hold our cookbooks. This addition added three feet of storage to the kitchen, by the way. The bottom, which was destroyed by water, has been replaced with a rolling stainless-steel topped table, and holds over-sized bowls and wine in the open bottom. We use the table to make bread and pies and to serve food during parties. Mort added an electrical outlet on the wall here, too, so making dough is easier because all of my needed tools are already together.

Though our kitchen cabinets are white, we stained the upper cabinet in a dark wood. Since we bought the table with the dark stain we approximated the same stain color when we refinished the upper buffet top. Through this color choice, we made sure that these two pieces matched each other and work aesthetically together compliment the kitchen cabinets. The record cabinet, which is also in the kitchen, has a darker stain that made it easy for us to use it. It had the needed storage, a great compact size, and the right color wood going for it. Obviously, we could have made it work regardless of its color, but in this case it was easy.

Our original kitchen did not have modern cabinets; they were birch plywood built as large units that ran along the wall and their layout felt awkward. Our first move was to paint the cabinets white instead of the discolored orangey brown the old varnish had become. This worked as a stop-gap measure, but we knew that our dream kitchen would contain different cabinets altogether. One day we unexpectedly arrived at a yard sale that was selling white melamine cabinets for only $200. My preference in my perfect kitchen plan was for off-white, traditional units, but this bargain was too good to pass up. In fact, it was such an amazing bargain that we bought the cabinets even though we weren't even ready to do the kitchen at the time. We were not in really good financial shape and when I realized how much mess, chaos and work this project would mean for the next several months, I froze. I stood in the driveway of the house, with Mort very excitedly telling me this would be great fun and a good distraction, and I just kept blinking and not saying anything. See, I knew that yard sales are not like department stores where what you want is there all the time to buy when you have the money. It could be years before we found a similar deal! I recovered from my panic, seized the opportunity, and lived to be glad that I did.

Kitchen Lighting

There are four types of lighting the kitchen. They are task lighting, under cabinet lighting, recessed lighting and pendant lighting. You are handling knives and fire in this room. Make it bright in here! Lighting in the kitchen is really important; one bulb or a single ceiling fixture isn't enough. Instead, 2.5 to 3 watts of light per square foot of kitchen is recommended (TTFWEB, 2006, ¶ 4).

Recessed lighting is a term that refers to the light that is in the ceiling. It is usually placed so that its focus is close to the counter, but it will not provide enough light when you are working paring veggies. That's

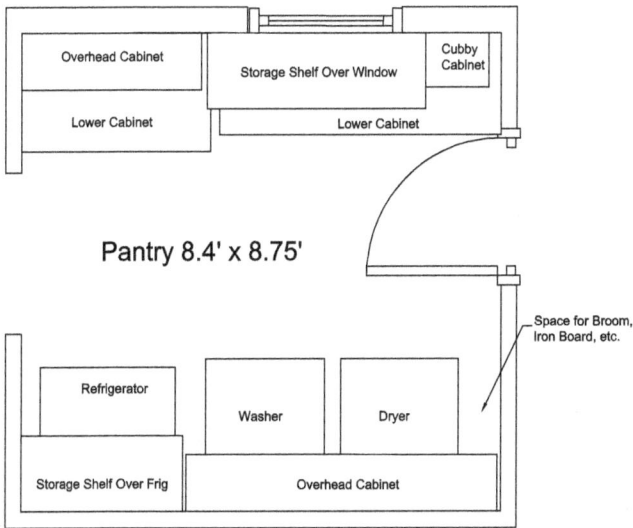

Pantry Drawing

the purpose of under cabinet and task lighting. Cabinets are going to probably block light from the ceiling and under cabinet lighting is the solution that you use to light the inevitable shadows. Pendant lighting refers to chandelier or pendant fixtures that make the room feel warm and inviting and may also be used over the sink or island. They are hung where they can be seen and add illumination as well as design elements to the room.

Kitchen Pantry

I look at a pantry as a place to store small appliances and other items and it figures right into my ideas about efficiency. You might find space for a pantry either in an adjacent mud room, miscellaneous storage room, or even a dining room. In the latter case, you might jazz up the look by making an upper storage area resemble a display cabinet, with glass doors or open shelves like a hutch, and have closed lower cabinets to store less aesthetically pleasing items like cans of soup or boxes of pasta. If you are recycling cabinets from another room to use as a pantry, you might cut out the bulk of the wood on the cabinet doors and replace it with plain glass. You could even splurge and get reeded glass or some kind of art glass to add a detail to make the basic cabinetry shine.

In our case, the pantry is really just a hallway that houses the washer and dryer and a spare refrigerator that we lovingly call the beer refrigerator. We enhanced its utility by lining it with cabinets with every surface faced with storage. We also added a sub pantry for appliances and recycling with five feet of cabinetry under a window. Most of the cabinets that we used for both pantry areas were formerly in the kitchen. We painted them white and gave them new handles. At my request, Mort also cut out most of the wood from the doors of the upper cabinets and replaced them with glass in a reverse frosted pattern that echoes the cookbook cabinet in the kitchen. We also added flat-front, two melamine cabinets, to take advantage of all the possible storage.

Summary: Economize
Here are some basic tips to keep in mind when you start thinking about the least expensive kitchen remodel for you.
- If you are hoping to keep costs down, do as much of the work yourself as you can. You may have to purchase materials, but

you won't have to pay for labor, which is estimated at 30% of the overall price.

- Keep plumbing, electrical and gas lines in place. That will limit placement of new components, but it will also save you money otherwise spent relocating those important items. Mort has the willingness and the capability to move these items and you may, too. But moving these items is a hassle and has costs involved, so think before you make this move.

- Walls and support beams are another potentially costly change. You may be thinking that expanding your room is a divine idea. It may be, but keep in mind that certain walls might be holding up the second floor and the roof of your house, and moving them will be expensive. If you are not an experienced home renovator, get qualified help. Operating on a budget is important, but you don't want to compromise the basic structure of your home.

- Reuse whatever you can from the materials you remove elsewhere in your home. I cringe when I see home improvement shows where cabinets are broken as they are removed from a kitchen or bath during a remodel. EEK! Those cabinets, sinks or mirrors might be usable somewhere else in a different configuration or painted a new color. You might want to use wood in an entirely different way, even for a kid's playhouse or tree house. Even if you don't want to reuse the materials yourself, they can be recycled at a yard sale, turning potential garbage into cash that you can then use for more improvements.

- Shop yard sales for gently-used, inexpensive appliances.

- Consider a dresser for a kitchen island—drawers provide great storage!

- Shop around for closeouts or special orders that were returned by customers. You can frequently get items such as these at a significant discount.

- Check classified ads, salvage stores and websites like www.craigslist.com for good deals. We found an electric, one-year-old, glass, black cook top for our island for $125!

The chandelier, solid brass and painted in a hammered pewter paint was free; the cabinets are the kitchen's original jazzed up with paint, doors cut and with glass inserted which was slightly frosted. The shelf above the window holds trays and decorative platters, the cabinetry under the window has recycled newspapers and small appliances. The window

Transitional Beautification for the Kitchen

We didn't expect and in fact were not able to radically change our kitchen for years after we bought our house. Knowing that, we made provisions to alter it with paint soon after moving in. You can do this too, saving your file clippings for the "someday" renovation plans, but making small changes to the kitchen's colors, cabinets, lighting, or other features to live beautifully long before you have the resources to make more expansive changes.

For example, the cost of painting for several colors is under $100; for that cost and some minimal effort you can be less annoyed immediately. Long before we attempted major renovations, we painted the existing orangey birch cabinets in the kitchen a creamy white and painted over the avocado and tangerine wallpaper - yes, we painted right over the wallpaper. The changes weren't meant as a long-term solution, but we reasoned that this cheap change would make the room feel better for two to five years.

Don't be afraid to make the same kind of short-term changes. For the cost, which is very small no matter your budget, you could change the room every year, if you wanted. Anytime we have moved into a house, we made quick paint changes to every room – we did this with permission if we were renting - to make the space our home. Once you have the tools and the ability, it seems crazy to ignore the satisfaction that this small step can have for your sense of coziness.

Did you know you can even buy appliance paint? We bought a refrigerator for $5 at a yard sale after our expensive fridge gave up the ghost. We used appliance paint and took the unit from gold to black—perfect!

Other simple changes include changing door pulls to something more your style. These might also be reused when you do the more complete change to the room.

Windows add light and warmth to a kitchen. Storage can also add a beauty and homey quality to a room. We tied windows and storage together by adapting an idea that I'd seen on a home tour. In Camden, Maine every July, the Camden Garden Club hosts a fundraising event. I mark this event, the Camden House and Garden Tour, on my calendar each year and going to it represents a little day of vacation for me. During the tour one summer I got an idea for modifying one of the designs that I saw and when I got home I asked Mort to put a wire shelf above the pantry window as a kind of valance. I have a collection of platters and by arranging them on the shelf, we created both an interesting storage option and an arrangement that allows me to enjoy my collection.

Tile can be beautiful and expensive. I chose good quality tile for our counters, but I spent a small amount because I chose the simplest and least expensive option, an almond-colored, satin finish. The island also has tile; I would have liked a solid piece of granite and someday soon I hope I have a budget for such a purchase. But for now, 12 x 12 inch granite tiles were much less costly and gave me a granite counter top without the prohibitive cost of a slab. (I have heard that if you go to your granite supplier and ask for small slab pieces you can frequently get a great discounted price.) Our backsplash is decorative tile with a textured, European look that we found at the local specialty tile store. We got a bargain since the store had only a few tiles in this pattern left, so they sold them to us at a better-than-real-money price.

Several easy steps can be used to make inexpensive cabinets look great. Mort and I used detailed three-inch molding that we purchased at a yard sale to top the cabinets and to decorate around the ceiling. I also wanted to put reeded or some other specialty glass in the cabinets, but at the time we were working on it, I couldn't find the glass, so I asked Mort to make the glass look frosted. He first used a frosting chemical but he didn't like the look. He sandblasted it instead and the result is very pretty. We splurged on handles at the hardware store, but, what the heck, the cabinet was free, and they represent the type of detail that make the cabinets look finer than they are.

To further customize our kitchen, Mort cut a rectangular hole in an upper, corner cabinet and finished it off with a piece of inexpensive glass and simple molding. I use it to display pretty glassware, brightly colored pitchers and containers, just like the ones I covet when I look through catalogues, but almost all of which I purchased at a fraction of the cost from yard or estate sales.

Mort also made a fun change to the pantry through a find at the dump: a Revere-style chandelier. It originally had a brass finish but he painted it with hammered pewter paint and it looks amazing!

These simple changes can make huge differences in the overall look of your home, enhancing the way that you feel about each room and the time that you spend there. Better yet, they can be made easily and without the investment of time or money needed for even a budget renovation.

Kitchen Worksheet

- Consider making transitional changes to the kitchen while you ponder more expansive alterations.
- For maximum effect of transitional changes, concentrate on large surfaces such as cabinets, walls and old appliances.
- Get simple ideas by touring houses through local non-profit fund-raising events.
- Continue to collect pictures to further fuel your imagination and vision.
- Take a class or learn a skill that will assist you in a future renovation.
- Always remain on the lookout for beautiful and functional storage solutions for coats, backpacks, muddy shoes, baking gear, etc. that would translate into utilitarian solutions for the specific spaces in your house.
- If you find raw material, used furniture or other items that *may* work in your new scheme and are available at a great price, bring them home and store them in the already decided-upon designated area for their possible later use.
- Remember: if you didn't pay a lot for the item, holding on to it as a possible right choice allows you to continue to wait and see what other serendipitous options may come along. However, it is also important to combine your storage considerations with anti-clutter mandates. When and if this item becomes less desirous for your project, pass it along as a blessing to someone else or recycle it into cash through a yard sale or internet posting. Don't improve one room only to clutter other areas of your home.)
- Study various outlets for the type of materials you will need for your project, such as specialty shops (i.e., a granite wholesaler, cabinet maker, furniture outlets, etc.), second-hand stores and

yard sales; learn the best places in your particular area to get a great deal.

- Gather tips from friends and associates for end-of-season discounts and store this information for later use.

- Read magazines for design trends that are universally appreciated; remember resale value issues.

- Always be mulling ideas for what you can do in your room, thus honing your sense of design and style.

- Keep your eyes open for great deals; once you start to do this, you'll be surprised how much you will find.

Quick Tips for Kitchen Planning

- Have a general plan, but be flexible so that you can adapt when you serendipitously find unexpected bargains.

- Know yourself. Prioritize your spending on the items that you really want and splurge on those things.

- Take your time—bargains are worth the wait!

- Know the items that provide the most bang for your re-do buck.

- Remember, if you make a mistake or change your mind, you can always hire someone to finish what you started.

- If you plan on selling the house, make wise remodeling decisions dictated by potential resale value. If not, please yourself!

• •

Now we'll look at the next important room in your house, the Living Room.

~ **6** ~

Living
Room

Whatever you call the room in which your family hangs out, plays games, watches movies and generally *lives,* this room is one of the most important "public" rooms in your house. It probably needs to be able to take a lot of wear and tear; if your living room is like mine, it's got upholstery that occasionally gets slobbered on by pets and mucked up with spilled snack food.

From a purely utilitarian perspective, an argument may be made that the living room should be a completely plastic-encased garage to allow for easy hosing down to keep surfaces clean! But that wouldn't be the cozy, friendly, and stylish environment that you have in your mind's eye. I'll discuss a couple of rooms in this section, the living room and the sitting room, which in our family is slightly less used. In your family, comparable rooms might be a den, living room, formal parlor or other spaces that serve the same general function.

Considerations and Planning

The primary question that we address with regard to these rooms is how we can combine the multiple uses and needs of your family with the beauty that you crave. There are several factors that need to be considered:

- How is the space used?
- How many people use the space?
- Are there multiple functions as we discussed above, such as games and TV?
- Do you have pets? Do these pets shed?
- Is there an exterior entry door off this room, so that kids, pets and guests are running from the yard directly into the space?

Don't feel overwhelmed by the questions; we'll address them one by one.

First, it is important to consider the implications of an exterior door that is connected to the living room. We do and when we considered the best flooring for the room, we recognized that we had to take that door, and the ensuing constant mess from outdoors, into consideration. Where I live in Maine, winter brings snow; that means that wet boots and shoes track all kinds of mess into the room. Even in the summer we get bits of the outdoor migrating inward, with grit, small stones, dust and dirt from bare feet, sandals, and the big old boots my husband wears. We also had to consider the other ways that we use the room. It has a large fireplace and we bring wood for it in from outside. We also clean up excess ash and bring that back outdoors. We decorate with plants in the winter so we had to plan for occasional water spills.

Knowing all of this, I saw the problems with wall-to-wall carpeting on the floor. There was no alternative for storing wet shoes and I didn't want to plan on spending a great deal of my time fussing with carpet cleaning. Instead, taking these practical considerations into account, we chose to eliminate headaches and selected a different floor treatment. In this, we considered many possibilities.

We did not use wood, though several of our friends said that they would definitely have chosen hardwood floors for this room. Wood floors need protection and, over time, get "sanded" down from grit and sand and dirt. I didn't want to regularly re-sand or refinish the floor. I also thought that a wood floor might be too much wood in the space since we planned on using wood on the walls as paneling and shelving.

I was familiar with the pros and cons of wood because we do have wood floors in our kitchen. They are original to the house and the overall style of the kitchen is compatible with their more rustic' look (translation: kind of rough). They have been sanded, larger cracks have been filled (so the heels of my dress shoes don't get trapped in the previously over-sized cracks), stained and finished with Linseed Oil. We opted not to do a polyurethane finish and instead let the wear show.

This works for the kitchen, but for the more polished look that we sought for the living room, we ultimately chose tile, which we purchased whole-sale from a friend who owns a flooring firm. The main tiles are 12" x 12" and there are 6" x 6" black tiles placed in a symmetrical and historic pattern. We have hosted tours though the room in which 200 people have been in and out and clean up afterwards involves simply sweeping the floor. That's it. We have been very happy with the beauty of the choice and its ease in upkeep.

In a nearby sitting room, the room that gets bright morning sun and is relatively small and quiet, the flooring is pine wood, the same that is used throughout most of the house. The room does not have an exterior door and the wear and tear on the floor is less than that in the living room. We haven't used polyurethane to finish the floor here, only lin-seed oil. Polyurethane is like a coating of plastic on the surface of the wood. When scratched the polyurethane gets scratched, not the wood. Scratches eventually build up making the floor look less finished. Tung oil and linseed oil offer resistance to moisture and stains. If you have crawling babies, you might prefer polyurethane. We like the worn look of the imperfections and find that it takes several years before the sur-face needs to be refinished. We have large oriental-style rugs through-out the space to keep the sound muted.

The flooring in each room functions as a simple example of how think-ing through the needs and functions of a room will affect the design that works best for your family. This is essential before you spend any amount of money on improvements. Keep in mind, too, that your friends may not agree with your choices. Talking about design options with friends is fun, but don't get worked up about differences of opinion. It's your house, after all.

There are other needs and quirks to consider. Our old house has rooms without a separate pass-through or hallway, which means that part of both the sitting room and the living room have to serve the utilitarian purpose of allowing us to pass through to the next portion of the house. You may have rooms like this in your house. Our kitchen is laid out this way, but this created more of a problem for me in designing our sitting room. The room is a modest size and the pass through takes up an important piece of space, potentially cutting off the areas used for conversation, seating, and furniture placement.

It is also important to think about how pets or kids may affect your choice of materials. In our living room, we've used a variety of oriental-style rugs spaced around the floor; these rugs were bought at auctions, already well-worn. The result is fabulous looking and yet neither spills nor dog hair make us anxious. If you have – or would like to have - some expensive stuff, place it in a room that will have less chaos, such as your bedroom or a formal, quiet sitting room.

Maximize

I'm married to a man who loves equipment and at times in our marriage we have owned speakers that are nearly as tall as I am! I like people to be the most important thing in the room, so I had to figure out how we can enjoy large stereos and the apparatus that goes along with them, without being swallowed up by equipment.

To deal with this dilemma, we built storage units on either side of our fireplace. The upper part of each unit, except the units immediately on the right and left of the fireplace, is composed of open bookcases, on which we display our books and knick-knacks. The lower portion has doors so that we can keep handy—and hidden—the TV, DVD player and cable box, as well as less attractive books, and kids stuff such as toys, coloring books and games.

The storage needs for the sitting room are limited and are accommodated with the use of a small dresser as a side table and a side board that I would like to replace with piece that has closed storage to the floor. That piece will be coming home with me when I find the happy meeting of style and price. We also used nooks in the room to place a wood file cabinet that holds all of the design files that I've discussed in this book.

Since the cabinet is a dark wood, it isn't really noticeable that it's a file drawer.

Ell removed with floor joists exposed. These joists will be used later for the Gazebo and the Pergola.

Can you put something on either side of your mantel? What about a dresser tucked in that nook and open shelving above? Are the measurements of the nooks and crannies in this room fairly standard? You may be able to buy ready-made shelving units; these often come in 30-inch standard widths and can be left open or covered with drapery or curtains to conceal any disorder.

What about a window seat? That would add character, seating and storage to your sitting room. You could put shelving around that window seat and have an entire area, a focal point, of cozy, comfortable storage in the room.

Do you have awkward space in your room where you could build closed storage? Built-in storage is a favorite of home buyers. Is it any wonder? We all have plenty of stuff—and kids have lots and lots of little stuff. Collecting it inside a basket or box and storing it within open or closed shelves is great.

Collections displayed can also add beauty and warmth to the room. Our open shelves in the living room are lined with books. With the fireplace, a view of the garden and the open shelves of books is it any wonder that this room is always the one people say is their favorite place in our house?

Economize
There are several meanings included within the term economize. One way to think of this is to minimize the things in the room, and in doing that you then economize clutter and create a better space.

If the room has become full of the kids' toys, is there another place to store them? Are the kids old enough to have most of their toys in their room and just a few in the family space? I'm a firm believer that a room that is intended for everyone's use should be pleasant for everyone in the family. Allowing toys to overwhelm the space makes it less friendly for adult activities and will undermine the likelihood that the entire family will make it a habit to spend time together. Instead, make this room a pleasant place for the whole family by creating order for every-one and economizing the space by considering appropriate storage and utility needs.

Another way to economize is to make changes and additions in cost-effective ways. Consider furniture such as couches, chairs and side tables. If you don't have adequate seating for the way you would like to see the room used, there are several inexpensive ways to add seating to your room. Resale shops, yard sales and auctions are great places to find upholstered furniture. You can find all sorts of styles: tub, club, wingback and occasional chair. (An occasional chair is a chair that has an upholstered seat and a wooden or simple upholstered back.) Used pieces of furniture are usually very inexpensive. I have several chairs, wing back, club and occasional styles, which I've bought for $25 each. I once paid $75 for a chaise lounge at auction and bought another one at a completely different auction for $50.

You can update second-hand furniture with slipcovers, or by reupholstering. Even if you buy the slipcover, there are plenty of simple covers that can radically update the look of the piece of furniture and your room—and they generally cost much less than a new couch would.

To save money and because I'm game for just about anything to create a pretty home, I've learned to reupholster – and not well, so don't be intimidated! I still don't feel very capable at this task, though since I first tried, I have taught several others how to do this. It has been very much a story of the 'blind leading the blind.' But we've blundered through the task with surprisingly good looking results.

I've also made several slipcovers. For that project I bought a pattern. (I used McCall's Home Decorating #3278). The 'pattern' isn't as helpful, I thought it might be, but the instructions that came in the pattern are the best help for me because they walk you through terms and measurements, including where to start. It's as if you have a helper with you to take you through the process step by step. Each piece of furniture is slightly different, but this pattern walked me through the steps to measure the chair 'deck', back, etc. and then provided instructions about what subsequent process to follow - in between my yelling in which I wonder why the *heck* I keep doing things like this, I produced actual slipcovers that manage to impress people. When I flip the seat covers over to show my mistakes, they purport to remain impressed, too.

Another way to economize is to think beyond money. Will you reupholster a chair for someone who can build shelves for the house? Will you do the plumbing for someone who will paint your room?

Bartering is back in a big way! Mort and I bartered with our plumber to install radiant heat in the living room. We had purchased an engagement ring for our twenty-fifth anniversary at an estate sale. The ring had an emerald as its center stone and I wanted a sapphire. But our plumber's wife liked emeralds and he was willing to trade the radiant-heat installation for the stone! Think creatively about both the design and the mechanisms to get the beauty you desire; there is almost always a way!

Beautify: What's In The File?

Let's take a gander at the Living Room File, shall we?

In the Living Room file I've saved paint company ads with colors that look pleasing to me, as well as chandelier and sconce pictures I printed while 'window shopping' through magazines and catalogues There are bits of magazines that feature various switch plate covers in different styles, fireplace screens, dressers and other sideboard-like pieces. After a while I started to see similarities in the pictures I chose because the colors are alike, the furniture has the same shape and design, and the materials have things in common. I know that I am drawn to pictures of rooms that feel open but cozy and luxurious.

The sitting room is a quiet place in my house where I love to sit and eat my cereal or read a book. But the pictures in my file represent my dream of a fancier room. I have a printout of the reproduction painting that I'd love to one day have hanging in the room and magazines pictures of rugs and lighting fixtures.

What will you discover in your file? As you look through it for patterns, you will need to ask yourself all of the questions in the "considerations" section and then go beyond the practical, envisioning how you can best make the room comfortable and inviting. How do you make people love to be in this room?

In our case, Mort and I love architectural details that bring a sense of history to a room. Though we have an old house, the original design was simple and did not have crown molding or other interior details that we love. So we have added features to create a cozier feeling, including molding, bookshelves, fireplaces, flooring, and of course drapes and seating. Cozy is really the best way that I know to describe the feeling that these features add to any house. When we did the work of adding details we used the files to replicate the molding that we liked. What design, how many inches deep? Can we imitate the expensive molding by putting several standard moldings together to make one big chunky monkey? It was looking at the details of my pictures and searching for specific molding information and drawings that helped us create the paneled effect using simple plywood and several types of molding in our beautifully panel living room. And we also used the same process to stack the moldings that surround the French doors leading from the living room to the garden.

Details of your design can also help create beauty. Things to look at include focal points, items that make you happy by creating beauty and harmony and a sense of peace. Our living room's details are in the first things visitors notice: the view of our garden, the chunky molding that surrounds the windows and doors, the open shelves that line one wall and are filled with books. It took years for us to be able to build this room, years in which I continually looked for ideas in magazines a while on tours, squirreling away pictures and ideas for the room's potential details and design accents. I would show them to Mort, especially when we had to focus on our hope that our financial future would one day really be brighter. 'Let's dream,' I'd say as I pulled out my folder of worn pictures and get Mort's opinion on different rooms and their features.

Beautify: Living Room Details

Mantel

In the winter, the main point of beauty and focus is our large-scale mantel and fireplace. When we moved into the house, an ell, was in this part of the house, which was an extension of the original structure. Most of the wood was rotten and eventually the entire room had to be taken down. Eventually we were able to build a room in place of the old el and we designed it around ideas that I'd collected over many years.

We both liked a picture I'd collected of a concrete mantel. The scale, or size, was comforting because it was simple in design but large. It was stone color, had smooth details and rounded lines. It felt substantial, like we had plenty of money in the bank. Though we looked in antique and second-hand stores, at auctions and online, we always came back to this mantel.

The mantel was not expensive, or, I should say it was much less expensive than a mantel in stone of the same size would have cost. But shipping it from Arizona, the only place we could find anything like

The room is framed in and the chimney is beginning, with neighbor and mason, Chip.

this, was very expensive. We consider many things to make this work for our budget. We tried to get local production, we thought of making this enormous mantel ourselves. We looked into renting a truck to do the shipping ourselves.

Ultimately, after considering other ways to have a similar large scale piece, we opted for unpolished granite in the same dimensions as the original concrete design we first spotted, but at a considerably discounted price. We installed it ourselves with the help of friends and it is quite the focal point of the room, working just as our original vision intended.

We use a fireplace and mantel for our sitting room, too. It is a room that we use occasionally as its size makes it a more intimate space. There is not a lot of seating and its location in the house doesn't draw people into it, other than me.

You might think that a house like Mort's and mine, built in the mid-nineteenth century, would include fireplaces, but woodstove hookups were original to our house. In our sitting room we installed a non-vented gas insert and built a box and mantel from stock wood. Our mantel is

$25 yard sale chair needs to be upholstered or slip covered, I haven't decided yet. Bought in the present condition in which you see it, I draped the blanket on the chair because the lower arm has been ripped apart apparently from a cat. I wrapped a fabric remnant on the seat to make the chair's main yellow 1940's damask fabric coordinate better with the rest of the room's furniture till I get around to redoing it. The dresser was free, from the dump, and we painted a barn red after seeing something like this on a house tour and getting inspired. The doors on the bottom of the book shelves hold toys for visiting kids, including our adorable grandchildren.

made of plywood and MDF (medium density fiber, a good paint-grade material). Design details were added by stripping an old dresser that we found at the dump of its curlicue add-ons. Placed on our freshly made mantel, the unit looks as if it could be original to the house and visitors think that it is.

To give this mantel some detail, I searched catalogs that feature beautifully carved woods in shapes such as oak leaves and other nature-inspired items. These special pieces were expensive, though much cheaper than an entire mantel. When I showed my husband the pictures he said, "I've got pieces from a dresser that I salvaged that look sort of like that." To which I replied, "What? You have cool stuff hidden from me that I haven't seen or even been told about?" These details create feelings of warmth and comfort in this room and make people ask to hold meetings, parties and other events at our house. People often do not seem to believe us when we tell them that the details we have built have not always been there.

Walls

What about walls? Walls? Yes, in home improvement, even the walls come under consideration. Our living room walls are sheet rock, which we installed. Using magazine pictures for ideas, we paneled the room with plywood and made raised moldings with several standard-dimension woods. We experimented with several kinds of wood to see what would best take the stain we were using to finish our look.

The living room has paneling and many types of molding around the French doors, which open onto the terrace and our garden. We used stock wood and layered it to create a molding that would have been exorbitantly expensive if we'd had it custom-made.

By the way, "stock" wood is wood that comes in predetermined measurements 1 x 2 and 1 x 4. We always use stock wood in building any project because it's cheap and available. Stock wood is available in several kinds: pine, oak, cherry, etc. To choose the best type of wood for your project, decide whether you will be painting the wood or staining it.

Miscellaneous Detail Considerations

The details of the room matter. By details, I don't mean that you have lots of little collections cluttering up a room or space. I like less 'stuff' and prefer fewer things of nicer quality, or at least things that carry the *imitation* of quality.

For example, the sconces that presently flank the fireplace are aged cast brass that we bought on eBay. The andirons were from an estate sale. The solid mahogany dining table in the room was bought at a yard sale for $60; Mort refinished it and it is a lovely piece. We have a yard sale side board that holds our estate sale finds. We got an alabaster lamp in a yard sale for $7; it didn't come with a shade so I had to buy one! The shade cost more than I paid for the lamp. Who knew?

Furniture also matters. As I learned to reupholster, I also learned how to unify the various furniture selections with color, making sure that the slipcovers or upholstery have some color in common, even with as many patterns as I have.

For the sitting room, I sewed—badly, I might add—silk drapes, made in large vertical bands of ivory and yellow, to hang on either side of the large bay window in the room. The drapes are not functional and seams are clearly visible—if you lift up the hem, you can see the thread just *there*. These drapes are simply panels that would not even span the entire window should I wish to pull them closed. They hang simply to add color, coziness and luxury to the space, not to block out the light or create privacy. I purchased the two colors of silk, one sale at a time and using my trusty coupon, from my local fabric center. I hung sheer curtains beneath these drapes and their purpose is to create privacy.

We have some original art, but frames are very expensive. We often buy frames at estate and yard sales. We have purchased frames that were not complete or had chipped or broken detailing and used molding from the local home improvement center to imitate the broken pieces. The sitting room boasts of one such highly detailed frame that will be even lovelier when we get a print mounted in it!

Quick Tips

- It's free to minimize 'stuff' to economize. Empty excess stuff from the room to create a less cluttered space for the whole family. Remember, kids are learning to live in a world of grow-ups and though the transition takes years, the living room doesn't have to be all about them.

- Use closed storage for kids' toys, coloring books, etc.

- Look at magazines and books, and take available house and garden tours for solutions to common storage dilemmas.

- Look at pictures for size clues. If you tour homes when non-profit events occur in your region, you will begin to get much better at figuring out what the magazine pictures reflect. Many very expensively decorated homes use more fabric, art, and lovely details to create coziness. The more often you are able to tour homes and gardens the better you will be at 'seeing' the *scale* of a room's furnishing. With experience you will be able to duplicate similar features in your home. Follow the lead of professionals with a talent and vocation for their craft.

- Mort and I have made a hobby of touring great properties and have gotten many ideas by reproducing the features of beautiful homes on a modest scale on our property.

- Used furniture can be a great bargain. Don't be intimidated, be brave!

- Unite various furniture styles with color.

- Bartering can produce wonderful results. What can you barter?

Conclusion

My primary message is to be brave. You can do this. To get started, I got books out of the library to try to figure out what I needed to know. I spoke in this section of my difficulty and my success with reupholstering; well, I got these results because I gave it a shot. What the heck? If you only pay $25 for the chair what real trouble can you cause?

I started with occasional chairs since it was a simple matter to remove the bottom cushion and staple new fabric over it. My early, more complex chair projects were not very good, but I use those chairs in my bedroom, where only Mort and I see them. After all of this, I admit that I still don't really enjoy reupholstering or making slipcovers, but I like the *result*: furniture at a great price and plenty of places for people to sit—and they're much prettier and much nicer than plastic crates or folding chairs! (By the way, I even got the electric stapler that I upholster with at a yard sale...)

Whether upholstering, painting, bartering, or deciding on flooring, the results will be worth the effort. Making these public spaces beautiful will enhance your life and bring lovely serenity to your family and the time that you spend together.

• •

Let's go into the private spaces of the house in our next chapter, the Bedroom.

෨ 7 ෨

Bedroom -
Ah,
the Love Nest!

It used to be that we spent a third of our lives sleeping. Studies are now showing that we are sleeping less. Though sleeping needs for individuals vary, the National Sleep Foundation reports that most adults function best with at least seven hours of sleep (National Sleep Foundation, n.d., p. 1). Side effects of lack of sleep are memory impairment, higher risk of heart disease and high blood pressure and traffic accidents (National Sleep Foundation, n.d., p. 2). Your health, your memory—gosh, your sanity and the sanity of your family—depends upon your being rested.

There are many life changes that make sleep more difficult. Aging makes falling and staying asleep more difficult. Studies show that sleepy people eat more (Kovacs, 2009, p. 238). but when we sleep deeply our bodies produce growth hormones that break down fat. In a March 2009 Glamour magazine article entitled *Lose Weight While You Sleep* author Jenny Stamos Kovacs reported that, 'some experts believe lack of sleep is one reason for America's obesity epidem-ic" (Kovacs, p. 238). In Glamour's own small research study women who were able to sleep a few hours more, a few additional nights per week, did not lose weight, but they did lose inches! I don't know about you, but sleeping more sounds like my dream weight loss program!

The bedroom is FOR sleeping; that's why there is a big, flat, soft surface as the prime focus in most of them. A serene retreat where rest comes readily should be a required prescription for busy people. You don't need a lot of space to make this room the best in the house. Figure out the style that makes you feel the most coddled and cozy.

Do you have to empty the bed of clutter every night? Is the room such a mess that everywhere you look you feel reminded of the work you should be doing? Is your office in the room, with reports and papers everywhere? Would you please grab yourself by the ears, look in the mirror and say, "This is the BEDROOM." Now, resolve to give yourself a clean, comfortable and peaceful environment.

If you have difficulty sleeping, understanding the distractions that prevent you from getting the sleep your body craves will help you create a peaceful room. It is important that you then use this newfound knowledge to create a sanctuary that helps your brain wind down and relax. If sleep is especially difficult, use every tool—the correct light, lack of clutter, a soothing color, quiet, and fragrance—to aid you in finding rest.

Maximize

The effects of clutter vary from person to person, but in most people it causes stress (About.com, 2007). Clutter crowds you and makes use of a space frustrating and inefficient (U.S. Army Corps of Engineers, 1997, chap. 2). I don't feel that moving the same 'stuff' over and over again is an economical use of my time.

That means you can't own so much stuff that there is no place to store it. I'm not even going to get into the studies that prove we only wear 20% of our clothes. One promise that I made to myself is to keep only the items that will fit in my closet and drawers. I am a good discarder of clothes. I recycle and move items to eBay or donate to Goodwill. We sometimes use the craziest reasons to keep things: I paid too much for this; I got it on sale; I'll fit in this when I lose ten pounds; this will eventually be back in style. Whatever! In the meantime this item is taking up valuable space and we need to wear it or dump it.

When it comes to storage in the bedroom, I prefer to hide things away. I mounted stacked discount store drawer systems in dark "wood" between the hot water heating pipes and the beginning of the roof line as only two walls in our room are entirely vertical. The longest walls have "knee walls," meaning they go up about three feet then begin to make the inverted 'V' of the roof-line. The drawers are small but they look sleek and attractive in their pretend dark "wood" finish. My closet is similarly shaped. The roof line's implication is that at 5'2 1/2" I bang my head when there is still 23 1/2" of floor space remaining.

I don't like a lot of visual distraction, so exposed shelves are not my thing. In other sections of the house and office, I have open shelving. But in the bedroom, I want a simplified look with the focus on other details, like family pictures and the view out my window.

Our king-sized bed fits between a door and the wall, with room on only one side of the bed for a table. What to do? I asked Mort to build a fold-down table on the door. The shelf has a small rail guarding the edge and a triangular-shaped bracket; when the shelf is lifted up this bracket supports it. When I'm reading in bed I have a spot for my water glass and paraphernalia. When not in use the bracket folds on a hinge and the shelf lays flat. It's the same design as the back-of-the-seat tables on planes. Planes, trains, and RVs are great places to gather ideas for small-scale furniture or clever storage, no matter what size your space.

If you find that putting things away is a constant battle it might be that the room is "telling" you something. Rooms with inadequate storage solutions quickly become chaotic and require hours to tidy. You can spot problems by simply observing areas that are regularly in disarray. If items have no place to be stored, consider throwing out things that you don't use because you can't find them anyway or creating additional storage that might be more suitable for the type of item that needs to be put away.

Storage is limited in my historic home, so only bedroom essentials are kept in the bedroom. Extra blankets, travel gear and clothing care items are kept in three separate places. What about you? What might need storage in or near your bedroom?

Consider:
- Out-of-Season clothing and shoes
- Travel gear: suitcases, computer bags, etc.
- Sewing equipment, iron & board
- Sheets, blankets, extra pillows
- Handbags
- Grooming items
- More?

If you have a large closet you might consider using a dresser in the center as an island. The island might serve as a place to iron clothes and as a staging area for packing or unpacking clothing in suitcases; if you travel frequently, this would be convenient and might even feel like a decadent luxury!

I have a bulletin board in the closet. I don't feel like I know how to dress myself without pictures and ideas for changing styles specific to my body type. I regularly update this board with cute clothing pairings, shoe styles and accessory ideas, so that I can use classic clothing with recent style purchases to help me dress my best. I use every tool I can to help make my exterior as adorable as my interior!

Economize

I use what was once a desk, but is now my dressing table, fitted with a mirror, and the place to store and apply makeup. Nearby I have a diminutive marble-topped bedside stand as the overflow storage for bottles of lotion, perfume, books and fashion magazines. Shoes are stored in the eaves on an inexpensive shoe rack and boots are kept in faux leather boxes tucked under the blouses and jackets. I limit how many shoes that I own by how many fit on the rack. (Though I must admit, sometimes there are just few more…)

Where does Mort store his clothes? He uses the room's original closet and two dressers.

After discussing my storage options with several clever and creative friends and deciding on what worked best for me, I made that space be as pretty as it could be for a reasonable price. My closet is in the eaves of the house; it's not a walk-in closet. I pulled pictures of bedroom closet spaces that made me think "luxury" and figured out how to imitate that look on a budget. Dark woods feel rich to me so the closet has some plywood stained in a rich dark color. The walls of the closet are painted a chocolate brown to coordinate with the dark wood. Mort put a light in the space so I can easily see into the corners and find what I own and a rug remnant is on the floor. A plumbing pipe holds the hanging clothes. It was really cost-effective and its holding capacity is impressive. It's not going anywhere!

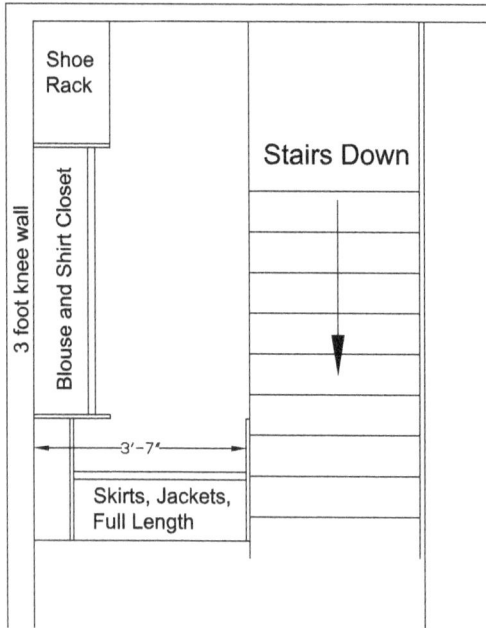

Marion's Bedroom Closet Drawing

(labels in drawing: Shoe Rack; Stairs Down; 3 foot knee wall; Blouse and Shirt Closet; 3′–7″; Skirts, Jackets, Full Length)

Beautify: What's In The File?

I have several files for bedrooms, including a Master Bedroom file and an Attic file; the attic is where the spare bedrooms are—or will be when they are completed.

The master bedroom file has magazine pictures of beds, chairs, colors, lighting and fabrics that give me the feeling of ultimate coziness; "fluffy but clean" might best describe my preferred style. I also have closet pictures in the bedroom files, one torn-out magazine clipping even has recommendations for adult and child closets from someplace called the "National Closet Group." Pictures of window treatments, window seats, wall paper and pillows are in the bedroom files, too.

For the attic I also have pictures of rooms with similar roof/ceiling shapes, and storage and bed placement ideas for tight spaces. As you collect you will inevitably see clever solutions for your house's quirks; save these pictures!

These pictures will help you to assess the type of details that you need to add to maximize the beauty of your bedroom. Details that add to a feeling of luxury can increase your sense of comfort and remove stress. You can add years to your life by doing certain things (like sleeping and relieving stress) and you could accomplish those things by making your bedroom a sanctuary, so let's do it.

Bedrooms are usually mostly comprised of "soft goods," fabrics for draperies, canopies, headboards, pillows, carpeting, etc. For those of us with allergies, there's only so much of that we can have in our room without having an asthma attack! Balance what you like with what will work for your life and your health.

Let's say you would love a fabric headboard. You could hang drapes along the back of the bed. If you have allergies, you may want to use washable rather than dry-clean only fabrics for ease in laundering. Or you could make a headboard by covering plywood with soft foam and then fabric. This would be an easy-to-vacuum option. These are all fabric headboards, just various interpretations on the theme.

As we learned in a previous chapter, emotions are influenced by paint colors. In the bedroom, particularly if soft surfaces need to be limited, color can be used to bring a feeling of coziness or airiness. Use molding details, mirrors and sparkly things like chandeliers to help enhance your space without adding more dust-catching fabric.

Texture is a way of bringing comfort and luxury into a bedroom. Besides the muffling benefits of carpeting and draperies, throws or pillows with nubby texture remind us of the cuddly and well-loved stuffed animals of our youth. Shiny surfaces can feel cold, but rough textures give the perception of warmth (U.S. Army Corps of Engineers, 1997, chap. 4). In hospital nurseries premature babies are placed on sheepskin because of the beneficial effects texture can have on human health (Merino Inovation.Com, n.d., ¶ 12; MI Woolies, n.d., ¶ 10). So use pleasing textures in your bedroom sanctuary to help you feel restored and serene.

The original builders tucked a window into this room and over the ell's peaked roof line. But I couldn't reach it to open or even to touch it and I felt like the Count of Monte Cristo trapped in a dungeon. If you look very closely you can see a paint few lines that show my dream of a large flanked by two smaller windows in my future for this wall, all looking out into our wood.

I keep family pictures in the private section of our house. I once read that Queen Elizabeth keeps her family's photos close to her in her 'private quarters,' and that seemed like a cozy habit to emulate. The bedroom and the second floor hall hold many family pictures. To me these things make the space feel intimate and personal.

We decided that when we built the eventual addition, we would add a balcony off the Master Bedroom onto the new room's roof. We were given a free – and pretty leaky- sliding glass door that we installed as we made progress. We eventually put in an energy efficient unit.

Details: Paint and Lighting

Since the bedroom is the place to completely relax, choose a color that is most comfortable for you. In general, earth tones help rooms feel gentle, while blues and greens suggest nature and are popular bedroom colors because of their soothing effect. Purple or blue-violet, which produces feelings of introspection, may also be colors to consider.

Lighting carries a different level of importance for bedrooms as opposed to other rooms, since the wrong kind of light will affect how you sleep, which is the function of the room. You want to control light through the windows as well as have softer lighting to read by. Consider black-out fabric at the windows, paired with a pretty window covering.

Artificial light needs to be adequate, but not intense. You aren't slicing vegetables in this room. You might read or watch TV or have quiet conversations with loved ones. Be careful of the light from TV or computers as even small levels of light effect the inner clock of our bodies and can cause sleep disruptions (Mesquita & Reimao, 2007).

Mort and I have a strong overhead light that we use only for certain tasks, like sorting socks. It's bright enough to tell black socks from blue socks, but too bright for lounging in bed, so we also have lamps on nightstands, dressers and tables. For reading in bed we have lights mounted directly to the wall behind and above the headboard. We found these at the dump and I then refurbished them, topping them with sparkly beaded lampshades that I purchased from a discount store. They are beautiful, space saving, and oh so very functional.

Quick Tips

- Remember: you sleep here; create a serene environment.

- Keep clutter under control for your allergies' sake and your emotional health.

- If you have carpets in this room, think of ways to make vacuuming easy so you can do it often.

- A soothing color and texture are most important in this room.

• •

Next chapter: the bathroom.

≈ **8** ≈

Bathroom

Your bathroom has a big effect on the value of your house. Kitchens and bathrooms sell houses, so a redo of this room will significantly alter the resale potential of your home. While, bathroom renovations are very personal, there are trends in baths that appeal to a broad range of people. According to DIY and USAA the average cost for a 'mid-range' bath remodel is almost $13,000 and, of that, about 85% of those costs can be recouped in the sale of your home (Smith, ¶ 5; USAA, February 13, 2009, table 1). Even if you don't plan to move, you can modernize this room and improve its cleanliness and convenience for your family.

I want your family to still love you when the job is over, so before you begin your renovation, give the job some thought. Like the kitchen, taking this room completely apart could make your life feel hugely chaotic. Do you have a second bath to use so that your family doesn't end up 'going' in the woods? Is it possible to do bits of the room at a time? Can you make the relevant improvements while your family enjoys a weekend stay with grandma?

I have friends who undertook a total bathroom remodel and it took two years before the room was even usable. PLEASE, don't take on more than you and your family think you can reasonably do. These changes, when done well, can bring peace to your life, but the peace will likely never be recouped if years later you are still not finished with the room!

Part of the reason that baths are a bit of an issue is that they involve the same important issues of electricity and plumbing as the kitchen. In addition, they bring the possibility of tile work that has to be accomplished in a pretty small space. In one of our bathroom makeovers, we made the mistake of buying the single tub and shower surround BEFORE we measured the space. We soon found to our dismay that they wouldn't fit through the bathroom door and our "simple" project now required that we remove the bathroom window and its frame just to get the unit into the room!

Sometimes a renovation is motivated by necessity. When we first moved into our current home, there was no place to wash hands in the upstairs bathroom. Imagining my growing sons and the implications of this accumulated dirt on their health, not to mention the rest of the house and our social acceptance in the neighborhood sent me searching for quick solutions. In a catalog, I found the perfect temporary solution: cheap and efficient, if imperfect for my long term design. It was a toilet bowl lid that was specially fitted with a pipe that allowed the clean water that was filling the tank to run first into this little lid, turning it into a sink so that you could wash your hands. We made do with this until we were ready for more extensive changes.

Maximize

Depending on how many bathrooms are in your house, you probably need to maximize storage in this space. I grew up, as many of us did, with one bathroom for seven family members, so I know how tight storage space can become in a crowded bathroom. In our Master bath, we customized the shower enclosure, building it ourselves instead of buying a premade unit, which would have been easier. Why? Like the kitchen island, we wanted to make it fit our needs, maximizing the floor space in the shower while still having a few inches of in-bathroom storage tucked between the wall and the shower enclosure. It has just enough space for my hair irons and a few toiletries.

For the bathroom to have a spa-like quality, less is definitely more, so cramming storage into every possible place is only a good idea if you need the space. Decide what really needs to be in this room and move other items to more appropriate spaces. For organizational purposes, what you use here should be stored here. (Christmas decorations should be kept elsewhere!) In fact, because storage can be at such a premium, you may want even to consider what you use in the bathroom, relocating non essential activities to another, less crowded, space. For example, consider styling your hair in a quiet place in the bedroom, storing your dryer and curling iron in an extra dresser drawer instead of underneath the bathroom sink. The former desk cum dressing table at which I apply my makeup is in an eave of our bedroom. There are several reasons for this, but it is primarily because the Master bath is small. We have only one sink and mirror because of our decision to have a separate tub and shower enclosure. You might renovate that same exact space differently based on your needs and priorities.

Other storage options abound, if you think creatively. Consider filling a plastic basket with your kids' tub toys so that they are contained in a finite space and have their own "home." Or hang an open shelf or stylish cabinet above the commode, but be careful what you put there! It's probably best not to keep items kids need up there as they could drop in the toilet if the kids have to struggle to reach them, which would fall into the category of, "not so good." Still, it can work as a storage solution for things you need occasionally.

Once again, storage needs to be balanced with what *your* priorities are. I wanted the small Master bath to not feel too much smaller and so we opted for a pedestal sink to maximize a feeling of openness instead of using a standard vanity cabinet. The cabinet would have provided more storage, but it would have shrunk the walking space in this room, which would have been problematic since we use it as a pass-through from the front of the house to the Master bedroom.

In a large bathroom creating coziness can be a real problem. Textured wall coverings, lush towels and a bench for dressing that is covered with a cushy fabric like terry cloth may help warm up that space. A low hanging chandelier above the tub might make the ceiling feel less open and help the space feel snug. Check with building and electrical codes for your town; remember, safety first!

In one of our small bathrooms, we found innovative ways to make the room feel cozy without feeling claustrophobic. We enclosed the shower in clear glass on the two open sides and used a separate tub and pedestal sink to make the small walk-through room seem open and peaceful. When the doors are fully open, every available bit of floor space is taken up with something, yet the glass makes the room feel pretty spacious.

Economize

You may find a dresser to reuse as a vanity or claw-foot tubs to take the place of a tub and shower unit. (I frequently suggest dressers as the workhorses for many jobs because they are reasonably priced - $50 or less in my experience – and come in a variety of sizes, from tall and narrow to long and squat. With a granite remnant placed on top or tiled in ceramic, repainted, or stained, they can be used all over the house.) Better still, you might choose not to change the vanity at all, but simply repaint, wallpaper or add fancy molding to the pieces already in the bathroom. If your budget is tight, try having a professional reglaze colored commodes, tubs and sinks instead of replacing them. If tiles are in good shape have them professionally painted to transform the space for a very reasonable cost.

Since floor space in bathrooms is often so diminutive, you may find deals for materials that are just right for your space but too small to be of value to anyone else. The bathroom floor plan shows that our upstairs bathroom is seven feet wide, but with a tub and separate shower the room is in fact only a bit over four feet wide. We were able to buy a small amount of wide plank wood flooring that we put in the bath – this may not be an ideal choice of flooring for everyone in a bathroom – covering the floor for about $30. You, too, might find great deals from leftovers of larger projects in too small a quantity for any other job.

In another bathroom we renovated, we used three different sizes of tiles, all in gray. The floor is tiled in a 7" x 14" tile that we laid in a her-ringbone pattern. It makes the space feel like a garden. But we didn't *plan* this tile size. It was available during our trip to the salvage store and "we bought it when we saw it." (These famous words are from the salvage store's commercial.)

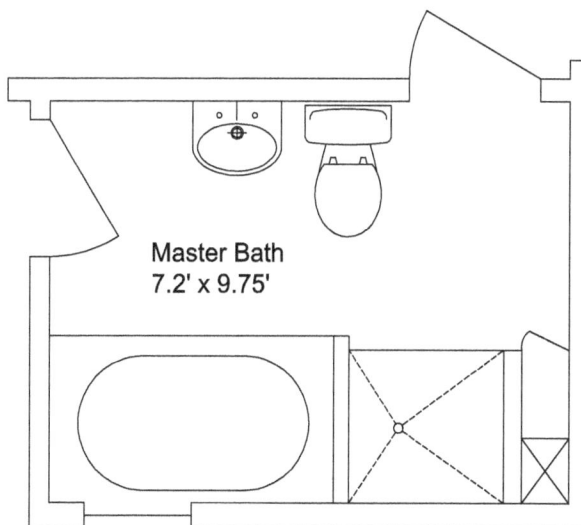

Master Bath Drawing

Unfortunately, there were not enough tiles available to cover the entire room. What to do? We used a 6" x 6" tile, also gray, though a slightly darker shade, to cover the little water closet portion of this large bathroom. The change seemed totally appropriate since the room has a door to separate it from the rest of the bath. Years ago at the recycling center of our town's dump, we picked up some 8" x 8" tile. We placed this between the one-piece tub surround and the ceiling. The ceilings are more than 8.5 feet high, so there is 30" from the top of the surround to the crown molding. We also unified the look by tiling down the wall between the tub and the molding around the little room of the water closet. We painted the walls a similar shade to the main floor tile and everything looks unified and tranquil. No one ever says, "Wow, you sure do have a crazy mix of materials in that bathroom."

Where can you look for deals? If you don't know that best places in your town for bargains ask around. Get to know local contractors. Find out what they do with structurally sound cabinets, vanities, etc. that clients no longer want. Scour www.craigslist.com and the Restore shops (stores that sell gently used and new construction material donated by retail stores and contractors to raise money for Habitat for Humanity) in your city. Check for close-out sales at locally owned and big box stores for items that you will be able to use in some clever way in your remodel.

Beautify: What's In the File?

Initially all of my bathroom materials were collected in one file called "Bathroom," but I realized that I'd like the master bath to be different than a bath used for guests or clients, so I made separate files for each. It's much easier on my brain and the patterns of my preferences and common styles become much more evident.

Sometimes the things in my files are collected because, and only because, they show an item or room feature that I can't figure out how to incorporate well. The 'Attic Bedroom' file, for example, features odd eaves and creative ways that designers have placed beds in nooks and crannies. My Master Bathroom file held an idea for another dilemma: a 30" x 12" sepia-toned reproduction in an antique frame that I picked up at a yard sale in New Hampshire. One very similar picture was shown beautifully displayed above a tub in a magazine that I found. I had loved the garage sale find, but couldn't figure out where to hang it. Voila!

I saved catalog pages that felt serene and had good storage ideas, a picture of glass tile that looks cool and fresh, ideas for bathrooms just for kids, and a small booklet of bath and kitchen paint samples from a local store. I also saved an article about the best fan size for a bathroom and how close to place it to the shower, as well as an article on color psychology from a British publication. The folder also contains basic instructions on making a slipcover out of chenille or terry cloth for the bath—yummy!

As you can see, I used some of the ideas that I saved; others lay in wait, either for my next file cleansing or my next inspiration. Along the way, I used these ideas to make each of the bathrooms that we have improved more beautiful, from the fixtures to the pictures, the gadgets to the window coverings. For example, I learned through much consideration that when choosing the fixtures for the bath it is best to think neutral. Imagine how lovely your bath would be with the clean fresh look of a white commode, sink and tub; you get a spa-like feeling without changing any of the other items in the room. Framing your mirror like a picture with molding can also add a luxurious appearance.

Reverse Roman Shade

Since your bathroom is probably a small space, it may be the place where splurging on a bit of granite, expensive wallpaper, or a special chandelier will have a huge effect. This small room could be a jewel box with one or two special features. We have used bottom-of-the-line basic tiles, sinks and tubs in many bathroom renovations, but have purchased higher-end faucets or lighting to take the makeover to the next level and make it look expensive.

In bathrooms we have used unusual treatments to maintain natural light and privacy. In one house within very close proximity to the neighbors we used deletion icy blue frosted glass to make an interlocking rectangular stained glass, replacing the regular glass of the double hung window. In another we used a reverse roman shade where the bulk of the shade was all on the lower part of the window and allowed the upper part to be exposed to light. In another bathroom we used simple frosted glass for the lower portion of a double-hung window. (Manufacturers have kits using a plastic that adheres to the window with water, or you could use spray on frosting or actual sandblasting of the glass to achieve this look.)

Creativity is essential! I once had Mort, God bless him, make knobs out of rocks. I saw things like these available for sale for more money than seemed reasonable. So we got our own rocks, finding ones we liked on long walks, and made knobs ourselves. To do this, you could use strong adhesive or drill bits specially made for granite, glue a long screw into the hole and attach it to your cabinet door.

Bathroom Details

Other items to consider include:

The Bathtub
For a cheap and really excellent redo try the professional 'sleeve' that is made to precisely fit over your tub and surround. For less than $1,000 it is manufactured for your specific space and professionally installed over the existing unit. The installation takes mere hours and the area is completely new.

Paint
Cosmetic changes can have a big effect without costing very much. Paint can be used to calm a too busy room. Changing the paint color to a dramatic navy blue or a pale taupe, or adding textured wallpaper or wainscoting could make a bathroom look updated and attractive. Mort and I renovated a 9' x 7' bathroom that had two doors and a window. I painted all of the molding and doors the same color as the wall so the openings were less noticeable and the room felt less chaotic.

Lighting
Lighting is inexpensive to change. Florescent lighting isn't flattering to anyone; full spectrum light could change the cute you reflected in the mirror! The best way to approach lighting in a bathroom is to remember the layers of lighting discussed in the Kitchen chapter. General lighting is to help you find your way; in fact, in a large bathroom, there might be two locations for general lighting in the bathroom, one in the center of the room and the other in or near the shower. General lighting is usually the main ceiling fixture overhead in the space. This single light will probably cast shadows as you peer into the mirror with the light behind you. The shadow cast from this light isn't flattering nor is the lighting adequate for shaving or makeup application.

The next layer of light is task lighting, which could take the form of a magnified and lit mirror, the kind that has articulating arms to move them to and fro. Alternatively, it might be two sconces placed on either side of the mirror to light your beautiful face evenly. Use full spectrum bulbs for the most natural light.

Quick Tips

- Make cosmetic changes for dramatic effect and low cost.

- Look for alternatives - like dressers - for an updated vanity.

- Check out sales online and at retail shops. Remember that choosing a simpler model of items like whirlpool tubs and fixtures can save a lot of expense.

- Look for material that is right for your small space but may be cheap because it is too small for many other applications. Leftovers at granite sites or installers might be perfect for your needs.

- Update lighting for a better-looking you.

- Be creative with window coverings.

• •

Now that we have the interior space started, let's look at the science of happiness and how that relates to your home improvement efforts, both from a décor perspective and in terms of living beautifully within a financially sound budget.

❦ 9 ❦

Health
and
Happiness

I want to be healthy and happy and I'd like to achieve these benefits while sitting in the sun and eating a tasty snack. Chocolate, preferably. by the beach, sans bugs and sand. Let's face it: I want as many good things in the world as I can get and in an ideal world, I'd like to achieve them effortlessly.

Still, I've been around long enough to know that rewards usually don't just fall from the sky; we have to work for them, envision the life that we want and prioritize in a way that makes it happen. And though we joke about the chocolate and the passive rest on the beach, another reality of life is that we obtain satisfaction from the efforts that we make to achieve that which we desire. This very effort of imagining and then working toward the new world that we imagine is an important part of being happy and healthy.

Another extremely important element associated with health and happiness has to do with the amount of time that we interact with nature. For some people, nature is defined as wilderness and they will spend dirty weeks tramping about in the mountains. For others, the time that we spend in the gardens that are attached to and part of our homes provides the same essential contact with nature, without the dirt and body odor.

How much health and happiness can be achieved in the garden? Study after scientific study show that every one of us can benefit from nature, regardless of age, gender, ethnicity, or other differences. In many instances, these studies addressed the benefits of nature contact for people who were stressed or ill, but if these elements helped these people, they will also help us.

Light

Natural light has an ability to help injured and sick people feel better faster (The CollegeBound Network, 2008) and eases depression; long ago, even Florence Nightingale commented on its relationship to better health (Leaman, ¶ 10). Sunlight is also essential to regulate our body's waking and sleeping clocks (Leaman, ¶ 5, 6). In Europe the beneficial effects of natural light are so highly regarded that access to it is a 'right' of workers (Herman Miller, 2008, p. 4). Randy White studied the use of natural light in large stores. Employees and shoppers had very positive responses to the skylights placed in the stores, with employees asking to be transferred to departments that were sky-lighted and shoppers saying the stores with skylights felt cleaner and airier (White Hutchinson Leisure & Learning Group, 2000, ¶ 10). Even on a cloudy day there is much more light outdoors than inside (Leaman, ¶ 9; Brown, Ph.D., 2006, ¶ 12). Apparently, sunlight's not just for plants.

Nature and Kids

We've been hearing for a few years about the increasingly poor health of modern kids. But it's not just a better diet and more exercise that makes for healthier children. USA Weekend quoted a study that found that between 1997 and 2003, there was a 50% decline in the number of kids spending time outdoors hiking, walking or fishing (Staff, 2007, ¶ 4). This is unfortunate, since nature plays such a great role in helping kids become well both mentally and physically. A Cornell University study found that kids with lots of nature around them feel less stress than kids who don't. Some nursery schools in Europe emphasize outdoor time and find that though their students may initially fall behind their peers in specific skills, such as those related to computers and technology, the end result is that they are more confident, happier, and better able to achieve in a wide variety of life skills, including those where there was a temporary early gap.

The benefits of having kids spend more time with nature translates with special poignancy for kids who have been diagnosed with some of the syndromes that are becoming increasingly common. For example, kids with ADHD had the same effects when given 'doses of nature' as if they were given ADHD medication (Centre for Confidence and Well-being [Centre for Confidence], n.d., ¶ 2).

Nature and Adults

These benefits also apply to adults. An article in the British newspaper *The Independent* quoted research that found that simply driving down tree-lined streets reduced road rage (Wright, April 24, 2007, ¶ 16). That seems to indicate that even a short amount of time with nature can have a big effect – I mean how much time does it take to drive down a street?—and yet even a relatively brief exposure provides some relief.

Even looking at nature from a window is beneficial (Wright, April 24, 2007, ¶ 32), though getting exercise outdoors is even better than looking out a window. (Wright; Nature Reduces Stress, Jul 27, 2004, ¶ 2). This makes sense, since combining the physiological benefits of a natural setting with activity reduces stress, is believed to help develop stronger immune systems, and is associated with building confidence (Wright, ¶ 2). Furthermore, many studies have demonstrated that nature reduces mental fatigue for older people (Inclusive Design for Getting Outdoors [I'DGO], June 10, 2007, ¶ 1; Jennifer B, July 25, 2008, ¶ 3). Physical activity – obviously good for us – has even more benefits when it is taken outdoors. Outdoor exercisers get better test scores and have lower blood pressure, and city-folk who live near parks live longer (Wright, ¶ 7).

Relationship to Home Improvement

In short, digging in the garden is good for you – and not simply because it is physical activity. According to the UK paper *The Independent*, scientists theorize that even the bacteria in the earth's soil may encourage the release of serotonin in our brains, giving us a natural boost of happiness. The UK charity Thrive promotes gardening for people with disabilities, calling their work, 'therapeutic horticulture' (Wright, April 24, 2007, ¶ 11, 12).

Flowers

I like flowers. I feel happy when I look at a bouquet that a friend or loved one has given me. But until I started to do some research, I didn't realize that these feelings are common. According to a Kansas University study, patients recovering from abdominal surgery needed less medication and reported less stress if their room included a flowering plant (True II, n.d., ¶ 6).

Other studies affirm the positive effects of flower on people, even in comparison to other commonly desired and appreciated items. For example, scientists measured how big a smile women had when receiving different gifts: flowers, a fruit basket and a candle. Everyone who received a gift smiled, but the biggest smiles came from those who received flowers. Days afterwards, those women who received flowers were 'significantly' happier than those who received the other gifts (Munger, 2008, ¶ 6).

These effects are not limited to women, for both men and women have positive responses to flowers. Studies show that flowers at the workplace positively affect the mood of customers and employees and increase productivity, social interaction and problem solving (John E. Williams, EzineArticles, n.d., ¶ 7).

Fragrance

Fragrance is a complex concept. For instance, 'clean' is a smell that firms such as Proctor & Gamble spend a lot of time and money exploring. We might think that 'clean' equals no odor, but we actually expect a bit of a scent to really believe something is clean (Byron, 2009, p. A1).

An article in Vogue magazine informed me about *table hold*. This is the art and science used by fragrance experts to create scents in the public spaces of Wynn resorts, thereby adding another element encouraging customers to stay, be happy and potentially spend more money (Stein-garten, 2009, p. 461).

The money that big firms have invested confirms that fragrance has an important place in our lives, even if we don't fully realize it. Though the study of fragrance is relatively young, it has already produced interesting findings. Researchers at The Sense of Smell Institute found that scent connects to our emotional receivers so that certain smells can change our mood. Their studies have found that floral scents create happy responses and (Haviland-Jones, Ph.D. & Wilson, Ph.D., p. 3) we recognize that we like to be with a person or in a place that has that fragrance.

• •

✎ 10 ✎

In the Garden

Where is all of this discussion of health and happiness, nature and fragrance leading us? What does this mean to you and your family? It means that it is good for you to have a tidy yard; there are benefits that go deeper than simply raising the resale value of your home, though that is also important. Simply sitting and relaxing in this space can bring peace and joy. How cool is that?

Let's be clear right from the start, I like sitting in my garden; sometimes I use a bit of hyperbole to make my point: "Hi, my name is Marion and I'm a garden addict." Please notice that I said that I like *sitting* in my garden. I don't want to dig or shovel. I don't like getting dirty, or sweating—eeew. I just want, and for my mental health I *need*, the yard to be pretty. If I need to dig and plant and weed and haul things to make that happen, well, okay. I'll do that. So, like the rest of this book, the garden chapter is about living beautifully through making improvements, not tinkering for the sake of change, love of dirt, or any such nonsense.

The evidence on the significant health benefits of nature has a name and even its very own official hypothesis. More importantly, it has a direct connection to this book's theme, for living beautifully means living well, in good mental and physical health. The biophilia hypothesis suggests that our healing response to nature is in our genes, wired into us. Hospitals are increasingly using biophilic design, incorporating nature when building new facilities. Years ago I read about research that found a significant difference between recovery speed in patients who viewed trees and nature from their hospital window and that of patients whose view was of a brick wall. That evidence has been restated in other articles (Joseph, ¶ 10), so by incorporating the natural world into your daily life and spending time making your garden beautiful, you will take broad strides toward creating a healthy life for you and your family.

Healing gardens are a concept developed as a response to this research. The goal in healing gardens is to produce a place that makes "people feel safe, less stressed, more comfortable and even invigorated." (University of Minnesota, n.d., ¶ 3) Wouldn't you like your yard to feel like that? Whether we realize it or not, most people feel cozy in outdoor places that resemble inside spaces: walls of trees, shrubs or rock; canopies of trees; ground that is like a carpet, allowing you to walk without tripping on things; and a secure place for your chair. In this section, I offer suggestions for using whatever space that you have to achieve this effect, incorporating your own preferences into an outdoor design that reflects the healthiest and loveliest environment for your unique tastes and preferences.

Maximize

A home is often a family's largest asset. When a home's value is estimated, the exterior condition and landscaping is the first clue to what you'll find inside. By designing the property surrounding your home to draw you out into a seated area, you add value because you increase the square footage of your available living space.

Since winter is a serious season here in Maine, it is nice to have garden elements that are visible through the snow in the cold months. Sometimes called 'the bones' of the garden, these elements are known as "hardscape." Hardscape is the fence, stone wall, or fountain that gives your garden structure. If it's an arbor or a gate it provides an entrance; if it's a pergola it may provide a covering. Hardscape contributes to a feeling of safety and coziness in the garden and it helps to maximize the space available in the yard by providing a consistent theme on which to

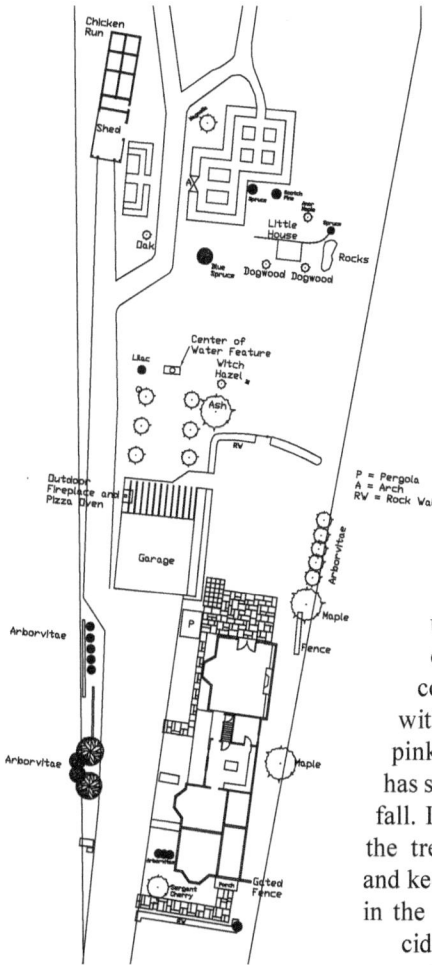

Garden and Hardscape Drawing

build other garden elements. It is used to divide spaces, providing a planting area that links and thus makes 'sense,' such as a picket fence leading to your main house entrance that now can be planted with flowers on both sides of the fence.

Hardscape also makes a height transition from the ground to the height of your house. In our case, we planted a Sergeant cherry tree in the southwest corner of our house upon the advice of a clever designer. The tree visually connects the towering building with the ground, blossoms with pink flowers in the spring, and has small fruits for the birds in the fall. In the warm summer months the tree's leaves shade the house and keep the rooms a bit cooler and in the winter, since the tree is 'deciduous,' meaning that it sheds its leaves, the much-coveted sun comes shining in the window.

Economize

You can decrease energy costs with smart landscape choices. A tree's natural cooling qualities can keep your energy costs down in the hot summer months. According to the Florida Extension Service, up to

30% of energy costs could be saved using landscaping to manage your property's 'microclimate,' which refers to the mini variations in temperature around your house, in places like a sunny fenced-in garden or a windy driveway (Meerow & Black, August 1991, ¶ 3). Shade trees can cool rooms, yards or black-topped driveways and make summer heat less intense. When leaves fall in the autumn, the winter sun is able to provide some passive sunlight and heat for your house.

I get other ideas for economizing every time I see a new garden or open a new catalogue. Because of this, I make a point of visiting the many homes and gardens here in Maine every summer during an annual garden tour. For those of you who have never gone on a garden tour let me explain the appeal.

Tours are generally held as fundraisers for nonprofit entities such as garden clubs or hospitals and include access to half a dozen properties with a variety of different types of gardens from formal to wild. Sometimes homes are also open for touring. These events are excellent opportunities to see in person some of the ideas that we see in magazines all winter long.

After a few years of touring you start to see features that are consistent from house to house, perhaps even some ideas you'd like to add to your own. For instance, I noticed the scale or size of the plantings or garden structures, compared to the surroundings, of hardscape pieces in the outdoor gardens. What are some of the structures used in the garden? There are pergolas, which are flat topped structures on which vines can grow, and arbors, stone walls and gates. Bridges and ponds are water features that pull you into to a corner of the garden. Over and over again the scale of these items leaves an impression of stability and beauty. They are not tiny or insignificant; rather, in my favorite gardens, they are larger than we would timidly do without thinking. A structure that would be appropriate in a 10' by 12' interior space will not be large enough for the great outdoors.

Because of these tours, Mort and I began building outdoor structures and creating gardens in our yard. Though I have tried, I cannot create these garden "rooms" without help, but I can add to a designer's vision, and I can tweak someone else's idea to suit what I'd like. So we have found and paid for the talents of others to help us. We don't usually pay for formal plans or to-scale drawings. We sometimes pay for sketches and plant lists, or I simply follow the designer around and jot down ideas as he or she talks.

The yard was overgrown because the elderly couple from whom we bought the house couldn't manage the heavy work. This photo shows the progress we had made from the overgrown state. We didn't take earlier pictures showing the overgrown condition.

Anyone who has bought plants knows that spending money on just a few plants can be very expensive, particularly if the plants are wrongly situated and don't survive the winter. It can be cost effective to have a designer work with you and make suggestions specific to your hardiness zone and the level of sun or shade for your site.

Inexpensive tips can be had from gardening neighbors in your town. When running or walking the dog in your neighborhood, notice the gardens in your community. Stop and admire plants or trees in these yards and you might make new friends, possibly gathering suggestions for your garden or even new plants in the process.

Your community may also have a garden club in which novices and experts get together to share garden interests. Such groups talk about composting, attracting birds and helpful wildlife, the environment, and of course, plants. Cost of membership is usually nominal and the enthusiastic help of some experienced folks will have you up to speed in a hurry.

This picture is taken from the bedroom once the ell was removed. The wall had been built but there was little else.

Beautify: In The Garden

The beauty of flowers can have a powerful effect on our health and happiness. One researcher said that women who received gifts of flowers reported that within just a week they "felt less anxious, less depressed, more compassionate and more enthusiastic at work" (Bailly, 2008, p. 197). Studies on happiness reveal that even looking at pretty pictures can change your mood (Bailly, p. 196). I know that looking through books on various styles of homes and garden design always helps me feel better.

I love knowing that the process of making my home and garden more beautiful is good for my soul. I have amassed various garden files in my efforts to incorporate as many interesting features into a flat, plain yard as can be reasonably placed there. You may have one folder, as I did when I started my garden file. Now I have sub-files for the front garden,

Change of plan! Mort split the wall and we did more clearing, planning and planting and added the Little House. That is part of the ell's original door, Mort and I designed and he made the stained glass, the slate is recycled, and I applied the fieldstone. The rest of the building we sided.

kitchen garden, and back and upper gardens. You might have a shade garden or rain garden, a butterfly garden or a veggie garden. Consider this a friendly warning from a garden addict… as we go on, you are likely to be subjected to an awful lot of exuberant enthusiasm!

My files include pictures based on the plants, topography or function of each space: rock walls, pleasant entrances, shady porches or sunny terraces. I have collected magazines pictures of parterre, formal or boxed gardens, (those with a border of boxwood plants), like those in Williamsburg, Virginia. I have torn pages from high-end catalogs with pictures of peaceful lawns and relaxing furniture.

 I have collected pictures of flowering shrubs with berries for winter interest, as well as photos of containers featuring plants that I had never considered in a particular combination. I have pictures of water features in tiny city yards in Boston, Philadelphia and Bangor with structures and plantings that were wonderful. I have pictures of fireplaces, garden ornaments, birdhouses and benches that look inviting and grand.

I have also gotten written plans from our designer so I can remember our original vision for our yard and gradually make the purchases required to make that vision a reality. For me, having a variety of different garden areas allows me to have a nursery for seedlings that have dropped seeds and begun growing either in wild places, like the driveway, or in places otherwise designated for the veggies, compose, seating areas, etc.

Planning Quick Tips

- When you get to know the neighbors, you can share design ideas and plants that are uniquely appropriate to your particular area.

- Join a local garden club.

- Start a file on the looks you love.

- Spending time outdoors will give you a health boost so get out there!

Landscaping: Economize and Maximize In One Plan

What is landscaping? Landscaping is improving the natural beauty of your property with plants, topography and features that provide beauty or have a practical use. It is making a shape of your property instead of having it grow simply where birds have dropped seeds or kudzu has spread.

Good landscaping can significantly improve the appearance of a home, mask flaws and provide physical and emotional warmth to a home's exterior. Research by the American Nursery and Landscape Association found that landscaping generally increases a home's value by 7 – 14 percent (Classic Nursery, n.d., ¶ 9). Multiple studies show that money spent on landscaping brings a strong return, and for those who spend wisely or make frugal spending part of their landscape plan, the return on your investment could be many times the money invested (Classic Nursery, n.d.). Just planting mature maple trees on a property, can bring $1,000 to $10,000 of value each (Arbor Day Foundation, n.d., ¶ 4).

Getting Started

So you can see that there are financial reasons to improve the value of your property, but where do you start? What are you trying to accomplish? Did you just build a house and the ground outside your window is brown and muddy? Have you purchased an existing home and the property is lush but overgrown? Are you surrounded by the neighbors' stockade fences? Do you have drainage problems at certain times of the year? Are you situated in a noisy neighborhood?

Deep cleansing breath. This process can be simple and interesting or complicated and messy. I'm thinking you don't have the time for complicated, am I right?

This isn't a design book, but it can help you get going in the right direction. First, figure out a landscape plan. To do this, determine the functions of the yard and prioritize these functions with your family. What would you like the property to do for you, or for your family? Do you need a place for the kids to play ball, the dog to do his business, or a vegetable patch? Are you hoping for a place to grill dinner or sun yourself?

Even on a small patch of sod these areas can be separated or combined in an eye-pleasing manner. The more you are hoping to do, the smarter your vision needs to be. Just like on the inside of the house, you have to use your noggin.

Remember to think about the available assets that your neighborhood might have for you. Is there a ball field close to your house? Does the community have a pool that you and the family can use, saving you the cost and maintenance of having your own? Ultimately, you are the one paying on this property and that makes you the best judge of its use.

Once you determine the functions you'd like your yard to fulfill, start thinking about the way you want the property to *feel*. The goal is to place things in convenient places – such as putting the grill near where the food is brought out and will be served - and to use plants and other materials to make the yard look attractive and inviting, hiding possible eyesores in the process.

Maximize

In maximizing your outdoor space, I mean several things: maximizing the money you spend, the use and beauty of the area, and the resale value of your home. Iowa State University says that the cost of landscaping your home could determine 10-20% of your home's value! That study refers to the process of having someone come in design, plant and build everything (VanDerZanden, May 1, 2006, ¶ 1). But if you can figure out what you can do yourself, reasonably, and what might be best done by a pro, you can make changes cost effectively and have a functional and beautiful property.

Mort and I found the best way to make the most of our landscape dollars is to hire a professional to help us with the *plan*. Once the designer helps me with an overall vision for 'garden rooms' or zones, I can fill in the details. You may have different strengths; as with home improvement and financial planning, experiment enough to know what you know and what you can learn and rely on experts to fill in the blanks. The local extension service of your university or garden club probably offers classes on landscaping design, or they may be able to direct you to a Master

Gardener program where well-trained amateurs may be interested in designing your project for reasonable fee.

P. Allen Smith is an author I enjoy because he makes spaces filled with different and interesting elements by creating the garden 'rooms' that I so admire. In his book *"The Garden Home,"* Smith shows how he created many of these spaces on his property, which is an in-town double lot. He explains how to give your garden a sense of 'time,' or a feeling that things have been in place for many years, by incorporating elements like moss on rocks. He also explains how a feeling of 'enclosure' can be achieved by creating spaces that make you feel secure and comfortable.

In maximizing your layout you can camouflage the trash cans or an unpleasant feature such as a neighboring view of other buildings or electrical wires. You can also create specialized areas such as play spaces for children or pets or an area designated for hanging the laundry.

Indoor walls are already part of your space. By landscaping with a careful plan, you designate spaces, make outdoor 'walls,' and in doing so, actually create additional space, maximizing your health and pleasure.

Economize
One of the best ways to save money is to incorporate plants and materials that are already in the yard into the new plan. You'll also want to use materials and plants that fend for themselves as much as possible, unless you're planning on being a full-time gardener. The less grass you have the less you have to mow—unless you like mowing, which is okay, too. Your time, as well as your money, should be important parts of your plan.

This project can be done over several seasons and needn't be completed immediately. Take your time. For now, go as far in your plan as you're able or as materials are affordable. Get sections done so that you can see the progress each season and soon your yard will be the prettiest on the block. In any case, it will be your piece of heaven.

Beautify
There are many magazines and books devoted to beautiful designs of all kinds of gardens, from wild and woodsy to formal and fragrant. One

such book, *Homescaping* by Anne Halpin, gives great design tips on matching your home's architecture to your garden's landscape design. Halpin suggests garden plans, plant colors and materials that might suit your ranch, Victorian or Colonial house. For example, if your house is white, Halpin suggests that white elements would be a good design feature in your landscape plan as a way to coordinate your house and grounds.

Landscaping Quick Tips
- Determine function when making your landscape plan.

- Work with a professional designer, if you can afford it.

- Reuse existing elements.

- Take your time!

Plants

Trees, shrubs, flowers, and other plans compose the living parts of your landscape. Whether you are preserving native plants, creating a woodland path, or making a butterfly garden, the horticulture is the living backbone of your plan. The plants that you select will transform your garden, addressing style and function issues all in one. You may want an edible landscape, with blueberries planted among the daisies, or a bower of ornamental trees and flowerbeds. Trees can visually connect the height of a three-story house to the ground below and give birds a nesting place. The use of berry-producing shrubs will attract birds into your garden; birdsong may help to mask the sounds of any neighborhood noise. Remember the direct correlation between spending time in a garden and lowering emotional distress!

Maximize
A small yard space or limited sun can provide opportunities to blend creativity and practicality in your garden. Choosing a bench that also stores toys or garden supplies, planting veggies in among the shrubs, or using plants that do double duty by attracting – or repelling - wildlife and creating shade are all ways to maximize your acreage. Consider potting in containers, which increases the amount of space that you

can use for planting beautiful or yummy things, even if you don't have actual yard space. Buying colorful annuals every summer can be an expensive task, but you could maximize your budget by packing long-blooming summer annuals into containers instead of filling an entire garden bed.

To maximize plans, I think 'multi-season interest.' Use plants that have a long blooming season or that flower in one season and then when they shed their leaves, have color or berries for birds. Perennials may bloom for only a few weeks but come back every year after a period of dormancy. I add annuals, plants that are not hardy enough to 'over winter' in your zone, because they usually bloom for months and have great color. The length of time an annual plant will bloom depends on the plant and the zone, or climate, in which you live.

The pergola, made from plans and recycled wood from the ell, bridges the area between the house and the garage and is a beautiful focal point. The lead fountain was bought through a wholesaler and was badly damaged in shipping. We repaired it and this is the happy result.

Evergreens, in tree and smaller shrub-sized versions, produce a living fence, a green backdrop and a noise buffering quality to your garden. They also give birds a place to conceal themselves as they fly distances and perch or even nest. Plant varieties that will grow to be the right height for your space, so you won't need to trim them. There are many evergreen varieties and they are not all green. Blue (Blue Spruce and Bird's Nest spruce), yellow-hued (False Cypress variety Nana) and green (Arborvitae Emerald) varieties are available in shapes that are weeping, round, irregular and conical. Types of evergreens, depending on your zone, may include holly (in the north) or flowering magnolias (in the south). These plants serve a function in every season and will give both birds and your eyes a resting place. They also create living structure in your garden. Plants such as these are referred to as 'architectural' because of the visual element they add to a space.

Economize
Plants can be easy to share with other gardening enthusiasts, newbies or those with experience, since many perennials grow into larger clumps that benefit from dividing, which is cutting larger clumps of a growing plant into smaller parts. This rejuvenates the plants. Once your garden has grown full and lush it's easy to share and trade the divided perennials with neighbors and friends. These plants may also be available for purchase at your local nursery, garden club or church plant sale. Using spreading plants is a very cheap way to fill your garden with growth.

Another way to maximize plants is to use bulbs that will multiply, or "naturalize." Daffodils, for example, spread by themselves over time, whereas tulips, which are also a bulb, become less productive each year.

Plants that are healthy and faster spreading include monarda, or Bee Balm, and vines vinca and pachysandra. Monarda is good for cutting to bring indoors and place in a vase; it also attracts hummingbirds. With such diverse uses, it counts with me as a great plant. It grows in purple, red or pink and is a delight in the yard. Hosta, daylilies, ajuga and black-eyed Susans are simple to grow, practically care for themselves, and can be shared after they have spread.

Seeds directly 'sown' in the garden, such as sunflowers, zinnia and vegetables like beans, grow without fuss and will make a grand display. You can wind pole bean vines up a tipi-like structure—and kids love to hide under the growing vines throughout the summer months. They might even eat the fresh beans from the vine without being prompted to 'have their vegetables!'

Most of my garden space consists of flowers and I grow fewer vegetables. However, I have found that some easy vegetables to grow are also very popular. These include carrots, cucumbers, green beans, lettuce peas, and onions. Tomatoes can be grown from seeds – I usually start my own plants – but many varieties are available at hardware stores and nurseries. Peppers, squash, and radishes are also easy to grow, just read the seed packet for instructions.

Most of the important work for plants and especially seeds is in soil preparation. If the ground is hard as stone, the tiny tendrils of seedlings will not easily penetrate and they will die. Get basic soil preparation information from your local university's Cooperative Extension service for free, borrow a book from the library or talk to your local nursery. Prepare your soil so that the baby plants thrive. It isn't difficult or very time consuming if you start small and have reasonable expectations. Think: how much time do you want to spend caring for this?

I have saved money by starting plants from seed, propagating plants from cuttings, swapping spreading plans with gardening friends, and buying plants at great prices from church and garden club spring plant sales. I have also moved seedling trees and flowers from undesirable locations to spots that would better suit my design. Further, I have asked friends with property and plenty of trees if I could dig up little ones, replanting them in my yard. Perfect!

Beautify

When planting your garden, consider color as well as texture. Japanese gardens, for example, are overwhelmingly one color: green. However, their choice of a single color forces you to pay attention to the various textures of different sorts of leaves: shiny, wide, feathery and pointed. Other elements such as bark, rocks, sand and water can also contribute interest to a single-color garden space.

The main reason why I have worked with a professional landscape designer is that I want many varieties of plants and materials in my garden, but I don't want visual chaos. Working with an overall design allows me to keep the spaces organized, not looking as if I have lawn furniture, rocks and plants crazily scattered all over the property. (In our family, we call this the 'plop plop' style of gardening.) Tapping into such expertise may help you to avoid potential problems that you may not even have considered, especially things that may be specific to your region or your property. Erosion, drought, or the need for water conservation are some of the issues an experienced gardener can help you take into account.

Whether you ask a neighbor for advice or figure the plan out yourself, consider your needs. Plan a low maintenance garden by using native plans that suit your climate and that will grow to the size appropriate for your yard. Know what plants are poisonous for animals and children.

Gardening Quick Tips
- Look for plants at local sales that will grow well in your area.

- Seeds are an inexpensive way to start a garden.

- Visit tours, parks and your neighbors for great garden ideas!

Hardscape

Hardscape includes everything that is permanent in a garden, such as benches, fountains, arbors, gates, birdbaths, pathways and enclosures. Hardscape delineates the outdoor rooms of your yard and provides structure, even in the winter when herbaceous perennials are dormant. Adding hardscape does not necessarily mean a garden must be formal or complicated. When you move a rock to a new spot in your garden, you have created hardscape!

Since developing the overall scheme of my property is not my strength, we have worked with several designers and have incorporated a number of hardscape elements into our yard. What has this got to do with frugal living? Like the improvements that we made indoors, we have changed the outdoor spaces using recycled materials and hard work that has paid off. When visitors and friends sit in our yard, they frequently mention how interesting it is that we have segmented our yard into fancier areas by the house that transition to less formal spaces leading to a path through our little wood. Our property is full of interesting things to see, nooks and crannies to explore and inviting places to relax.

Maximize

Hardscape design takes careful planning, more so than the rest of the garden, or even a paint job on the interior of your house. You can experiment with flowers, which can be transplanted if you decide you'd rather have them someplace else, but you don't want to have to move the shed all over the yard because it doesn't work where you built it. With careful planning, you can achieve the right scale between the elements on your property so that your house and garden look like they belong together. Remember, just like spaces inside your house, your needs and tastes regarding your garden spaces may change over the years, too. The right foundation for your garden plan can ensure that it is easier to make cosmetic changes later.

Economize

Reusing items is always an inexpensive way to save money. Mort and I have recycled all kinds of things to create hardscape in our yard.

Our neighbor removed a dilapidated barn and gave us some of the wood, which, combined with salvaged wood from removing the ell off the back of the house, we used to build a 12' by 12' enclosed wooden structure several hundred feet into our wood. We topped it with a metal roof and screened it in; we call this our Gazebo! This structure is made almost entirely of recycled wood... and it was FREE! As the recycled wood fails with age, we replace it with purchased pressured treated lumber. We also built a pergola using the large lumber also salvaged from the El. To complete *both* structures, we only had to purchase a bit of wood, metal sheeting, screens and paint. Oh yeah, we also worked really hard to build them, but the financial outlay was very small.

Mort got plans from *The New Yankee Workshop's* TV carpenter, Norm Abrams, for both the pergola and another item he built, our Lutyens bench. He also got ideas from that show for the arch that we positioned at the opening of our yet-to-be constructed, fenced in vegetable and fruit garden. We live in Maine and rocks are plentiful, meaning free. As we dug in the dirt for other construction projects and especially after we removed the El, we 'harvested' the rocks we found and have built a stone wall in the yard that beautifully enclosures various spaces. Dry staked stone walls, constructed without mortar, are prevalent in New England. You may also have seen them on a visit to the British Isles.

We saw the potential - inside and out - in this beautiful home.

These walls are the byproduct of farmers who tilled the soil and found rock after rock under the surface. Since root tendrils prefer well-turned soil, the rocks line the property boundaries and eventually make walls. The work required hard labor, but it didn't cost a dime! (Ten years later, we decided we wanted to build the wall 20" higher; there were still plenty of free rocks available!)

At yard and estate sales, we have found bargains on needed tools and supplies, such as shovels and rakes, peony stands, wheelbarrows, pots, weed whackers, and wicker furniture. Someone once gave us some wrought-iron fencing that we spruced up and incorporated into our hardscape design. You may find garden ornaments, hammocks and all kinds of lawn furniture at these sales—all are bargains compared to a full-price purchase.

The granite curbing added the final touch distinguishing the gravel drive from the gardens. Designer Kathryn McCatherin helped us with the design of the structures that separate the side garden areas. The walls create additional places for vines and plants and allow us to hang lead and ceramic water fountains. The sound of water acts to camouflage street sounds.

Beautify

In my garden, the beauty is in the special details. Mort created a gate from the aforementioned wrought-iron fence that makes the back garden's walled space very cozy and welcoming. One day, he constructed an arch for that gate, from which he hung a light to frame the view beyond. This idea was taken from a picture in the file. Seeing it allowed Mort and I to decide if we both liked the look and whether the details, such as the light, might work well. We lined the path to our woodland screen house, the Gazebo, with slate that was being disposed of at a lawn center. One again, this was free. Mort crafted a copper weather vane for our gazebo out of plumbing supplies. All were copper, which is a softer metal, easier to work with. They weren't as costly as a Real Money weathervane and the material used can take the elements.

People regularly ask to take pictures in the yard and to hold parties and get-togethers here. The sense of joy and serenity that the entire place gives to us and our guests is invaluable.

Quick Tips
- Use items in your hardscape that are found easily in your region.

- Reuse and recycle whenever possible.

A Final Note

In these sections about landscape, hardscape, and plants, my goal is to encourage you to get outside, focusing on your garden as a beautiful extension of your home. There are many benefits to indoor home improvement activities; the design and implementation processes can build self confidence as you take control and the beauty of the end result will enrich the lives of your family and friends. Still, with the garden, the results are even more immediate, even more tangible. Just the process of being outside frequently will bring more happiness to your life and by creating an opportunity for your children, neighbors, and friends to do the same, you are literally making the world a better place.

• •

❧ 11 ❧

Garage
and
Other Buildings

Is a garage a good investment? In a cold climate the addition of an insulated garage can increase the comfort of your family, as well as the resale value of your home—between $2,000 to $10,000! A one-car garage is not as good a value as a two-car one, unless by building it you are creating parking options where none existed, such as in an historic of older neighborhood. Even so, if you are considering the construction of a one-car garage, don't spend a lot building it because the resale value is limited on these tiny garages (Jessica Bryan, AllExperts, July 20, 2006, ¶ 1).

Many builders have positioned today's garages to be center stage, with either one giant door or several enormous doors as the focal point of your house, dwarfing the home's front entrance and demanding one's full attention. Builders aren't always considering the confusion that a delivery person might encounter trying to find your house's entrance in the design or construction . I can only say that I have stood in plenty of driveways trying to figure out where I was supposed to go to find the house's entrance!

If a giant garage door is overwhelming your curb appeal, take a critical look as you may have become accustomed to what is a dilemma or an eyesore for others. Are the garage doors sagging or dented? Are they in good condition but just oversized? If you cannot afford to replace the garage doors right now, you might consider landscaping tricks that you can use to guide visitors to the door.

Maximize

Imagine yourself standing outside your house, maybe in the rain or at night. Imagine you've never been there before. You park the car and stare at the garage. Now what? Which way should you go to find the door of the house? Is the door visible from where I end up when I park my car?

Your house may need some tweaking if you face design disadvantages. Consider a lamppost to shed light or a big pot of flowers to mark the path toward your entry door. You could set a bench, sled, lawn ornament or water feature nearby to add interest or widen the path that leads to the entry. Alternatively, you could place an appropriately sized – not too tall that it blocks the view- fence that leads the visitor to the important entrance. Even a decorative flag can help first-time visitors feel welcome and confident as they approach your home. Whatever you use, be sure it will be effective if winter snow is in the cards. If you have a long walkway leading to your door, draw your visitor down the path with series of lampposts, a large welcome sign hanging joyfully or a curving flowerbed.

Economize

If building a garage is your plan, tackle the project with the ingenuity and frugality on which this book is based. Perhaps you can build in stages, completing the slab, then 'framing it in' which builds the exterior. We built our garage in this fashion and then had a 'siding party' to apply the siding to the building ourselves and with hearty friends with whom we traded various services.

Windows can add a lot of character and cost to any building. Knowing the plans we had to one day construct a garage, we bought new windows when deals appeared. In one summer we were able to score three new windows of various shapes that we stored and later used in the garage. Coincidentally, each window cost $25 apiece. That is a significant savings from the approximately $200 Real Money price tag and each of these windows were literally as good as new; they had manufacturer stickers still glued to the glass.

We economized in terms of both space and money by buying insulation for the garage a bit at a time. That worked out well because we did the installation on weekends and an entire load of the required amount of insulation would have filled the space and kept the cars out in the weather. This way we bought some insulation, installed it, bought some more insulation and installed that until the garage was done.

For lighting we used garage sale finds and inexpensive fixtures from hardware stores. Mort did the electrical work, which is permitted by code. If you choose to add lighting either on posts or attached to the building you could try solar-powered lights, available from many hardware and discount stores. They don't require an electrician for installation and the newer models are quite bright. We took a long row of cabinets that were designed to hang on the wall and have placed them on the garage floor. Finding doors to fit these cabinets took a while. In addition to "found" (read "used") doors, Mort ended up using material that was originally a long pantry door and cutting that to fit. Mort made more rock knobs for the cabinet handles and they look charming. He also got plywood to make a bin for my potting soil and fitted it with a large brass handle.

I store clay pots and a few more attractive items on shelves that Mort hung on the walls. He brought home a metal bookshelf and hung it up after decorating the walls with pieces of a pre-finished wood floor a friend brought us from his flooring business. We also framed a Bangor Garden Show poster for the wall. We waited for what seemed like a really long time to find a counter top from the dump or a yard sale, but ended up actually buying one, which gives me a place to attractively display potting items—and a handy workspace as well.

At a Shriner's yard sale one rainy Saturday we got three metal lanterns from the 1940s. These things are sold in high-end catalogs because of their timeless appeal. We only paid 25 cents each for ours! Mort had to update the wiring but, still, that's a pretty good price.

There was one other element that I wanted to add to my garage's gardening zone. In gardening catalogs, I had been seeing these very convenient small plastic sinks that hooked up to a garden hose. They looked practical, but they were expensive! Some time before, Mort and I had bought this quirky insulated stainless steel double tub for $10 at a yard sale. It had a hinged lid and it looks like it might have been used for ice cream in a truck. Mort thought maybe he'd put ice in it and have iced tea or beer in the garage, but I thought it would make an excellent sink. Mort agreed, installed a hose in a hanging wire basket for a faucet, and made a drain for it that empties into the side garden. Now I have the best potting zone on the planet!

The walls of the garage are sheathed in recycled wood flooring. The sink is fed by a water line and hose and drains clean water through a pipe into the garden on the outside of the garage. The cabinets hold gloves and tools and also include a soil drawer camouflaged as another cabinet. The lamps were $0.25 each at a yard sale.

Mort is happy too, though for a different reason. He has a cool riding lawn mower in his garage zone. He found it one day when he was hanging around the dump; a couple of kids pulled up with a mower in the back of a truck. He asked about the condition of the mower and was told that the father had passed away and a neighbor had tried to repair the mower, but it had been a year and pieces were now missing. Mort said to the kids, "So, if I give you $5 each will you drive the mower to my house?" And they did!

Oh, gosh, was Mort happy! What is it with men and tractors? The lawn mower need new tires and a carburetor but with $60 of repairs, Mort was up and running. He rides around the property yelling to me, "Come out and take a ride on my tractor!"

After God sent the nice lawn mower, we started to talk about yard carts. "Why," Mort would ask, tongue in cheek, "doesn't God send a yard cart to go with the riding lawn mower? After all, certainly God knows that a riding lawn mower is best with a cart." Mort checked the dump and yard sales religiously waiting for his yard cart. We both expected it to show up, and two years later it did! Mort was helping a neighbor who had recently gotten a new lawn mower. He noticed that Steve had two yard carts behind his garage, a new one he bought to go with his mower and an old, rusted-out one that Steve said Mort could have for free. Mort brought that beauty home, sandblasted it and painted it. Later, when that machine gave up the ghost and our finances improved, he was able to find a dandy used machine for a great price.

Beautify
I didn't have an instinctive plan for beautifying our garage. However, if this is your project, you'll find as I did that you'll gain inspiration as you begin. I found inspiration in many garage door brochures, learning that I like the 'carriage style' versions of garages with fancy doors and nice landscaping.

To imitate that luxury on a budget we installed very simple, though efficient, garage doors. The siding is white and the garage doors are also white and plain. However, we jazzed it up by adding a Palladian-style window, which Mort found for free on one of his treasure hunts to the dump. The window's frame is painted in an accent color, but it is the window that draws your eye and gives the otherwise plain garage a crucial design detail. We found a pair of carriage-style light fixtures at a yard sale and bought them for $10 each. They were brass and I painted the brass black and Mort hung one of the fixtures under the Palladian window from a large antique metal arm that we also painted black. It looks similar to a magazine picture that I was trying it imitate, but it was a lot cheaper!

To get even more of the detail on the garage face without paying for special doors, we planted climbing hydrangea to grow on trellises that are vertical to the garage. A trellis planted with Morning Glories or other fast-growing vines would have added a dimension, beauty and detail as well and provided vines for the cost of the seeds.

Keep in mind that all of your outbuildings, including the garage, should look as if they belong on the same property, so make them similar in color or design to your house. Our garage is the same color and style as the main house; the sheds and other buildings are a different color from the main house, but are similar in color to each other. Paint is also a relatively inexpensive way to camouflage, or draw attention to, features on the garage. If your garage doors are drawing attention away from the front door of your house, confusing delivery people and guests, changing the garage door paint color could be a simple fix. You could paint the garage doors the same color as your house and paint the front door a strong color to help visitors understand where you want them to go.

Zones of Organization

You probably don't have multiple outbuildings, so you need the garage to function in many ways: to hold lawn mower and trimmer, snow blower, planting gear, tomato cages, shovels, yard carts, kids' bikes and outdoor toys, sporting equipment, saws and shop tools—oh, and the cars!

Many people who have a garage use it as a "spare room," piling it full of poorly-organized extra items. That's a lot of wasted space to pay taxes on! If your garage is full of items that don't belong there, take everything out and ruthlessly donate, recycle or discard things that you do not use, make some space for things you do use and organize them carefully.

If you experience strong emotional resistance to cleaning out the things that have been kept in the garage, consider hiring a professional organizer to help tackle the project. As with a financial planner, who can take some of the angst out of talking about finances, sometimes it is easier to have a stranger rather than our spouse tell us it's time to let things go! If you want an organized space, do what it takes to get there, including being aware of your own limitations.

If you organize the garage yourself, set up 'zones' or areas to hold similar items. We divided our space into two parts: gardening things and the tools that Mort needs for woodworking and auto repair. We placed our zones where that person's car usually 'lives.' That organization reflects the way that we spend our time and you'll need to make a similar assessment of priorities when organizing your space. For example, if you use your sporting equipment very frequently, you will want to give it a prominent, easily-accessible spot. Make sure to take advantage of vertical space, using not just the floor, but the walls and ceiling. Remember who will be using particular items, though; for example, give your smallest kids the lowest storage area so they can—hopefully—manage their gear by themselves. If the kids can't reach the storage bins there is NO hope that they can do the tidying themselves.

You can tell what kinds of zones you need once you purge your extra clutter. Do you love planting and gardening? Do you have a lot of stuff for that hobby? You need a planting zone in the garage, or even a separate "potting shed." Look at the preponderance of 'stuff' to know what zones would be beneficial.

Living in snowy New England as we do, our garage can't just be a place to store overflow stuff from the house. It actually needs to keep both cars snug and protected against the weather. Furthermore, Mort uses the garage as a workshop and when he needs the space we temporarily pull the cars out so that he can roll out the tools he needs for the job.

Other Outside Buildings

Our outside buildings also include a shed that we use for the riding lawn mower, general storage and for the chickens; a gazebo further back in the woods; and the newest outbuilding, which we call the Little House.

The Little House's aesthetic purpose is to give a back to the garden 'rooms' before the property gets more wild and our wood begins. It is a small playhouse for children, 6' x 8' on a slab, constructed of new wood. However, though the wood is new, the rocks that we also used to construct it are from the property, the slate is all recycled, and Mort crafted the two stained glass windows from salvaged frames. Some of the glass used in the construction was left over from projects that we completed in the 1980s.

The yet-to-be sheathed Gazebo roof with Mort's all copper weather-vane. Made from a toilet float, copper tubing and copper sheet shaped into the topper and the arrow's point and tail. Since copper is a soft metal it is relatively easy to shape and the natural patina is attractive.

To decorate the inside, we bought yard-sale or second hand store furniture for a few dollars apiece, hung salvaged, but presently non-working light fixtures, a chalk board, and a fireplace mantel that we made from salvaged material.   It is a safe and pleasant place for kids to play and boy is it cute!

Beautify: What's In the File

I don't have very many pictures in this file though I do have a few of window boxes and interesting shutters, light fixtures, etc. This file is never thick for me because in my mind, the garage is more about storage and less about beauty, though the file does contain "odds and end" kinds of pictures. I keep ideas for nice storage for garden tools or tools here such, including one picture from a catalog that shows an outdoor sink for planting and potting things. I grabbed that idea for the little 'potting shed' area on my side of the garage. Another magazine showed tools prettily arranged on the potting shed wall, which I copied for our planting area. A third magazine showed a drawer that was custom made for potting soil. My clever husband was able to make a similar contraption that works wonderfully and makes me feel like quite a garden princess whenever I use it. The pictures of the sink, shelves, and tools that inspired the tidy way to beautifully organize my garden 'stuff' has helped us create a feeling of luxury in our modest garage.

The most important thing about the garage, though, is what to avoid. If you have a garage, or plan to build one, it will add very little value to your home if it is simply a storage space. Many people use their garages this way, losing even the space to store their car in the process. Unfortunately, especially in homes where the garage is designed to monopolize visual attention, the storage then can become the 'first impression' of your house, setting the tone for anyone who arrives, including you. By some estimates removing clutter from the family garage could add up to 25% more usable space to your house (JNK Products, n.d., ¶ 1). See the previous chapters for ideas about where to donate the things you aren't using or have a yard sale, followed by a stop at the donation center to get rid of what remains.

Quick Tips

- Make the entrance easy to find with lighting and paint.

- Make the garage a beautiful part of your home with trellises and other plantings.

- Chuck clutter and make room for the cars.

- Organize into zones using vertical space and easy to reach storage for kids.

- Look at store flyers, libraries or bookstores for entire books of storage ideas for oversized sports items or tools that are kept in most garages.

• •

Now let's move from putting some order in your house to putting your financial house in order.

∂ 1 2 ∂

Retirement:
I Hope
You Like Dog Food!

As I indicated in the introduction and alluded to throughout this book, I do not believe that living beautifully needs to mean living outside of your means. Bringing beauty into your life is a holistic process that includes aesthetic details of your home and garden, especially as they affect your happiness and your health. It also means achieving these goals with a wise eye always focused on finances. Beauty in the home or garden need not – indeed, in a true sense cannot – come at the expense of the financial bottom line.

This next chapter will help you to make sure that your future is as beautiful as your home and garden, by making sure that you are saving enough money to maintain both your physical and your emotional health. In this chapter, you'll see the other side of my personality, moving from my gushing emphasis on coziness to a sterner tone that I use in my financial analysis. Both sides reflect my expertise and personality and both are grounded in my conviction that we each have the capacity to live well wisely.

Looking Forward to Retirement? I Hope You Like Dog Food!

The future may seem far away and an odd place for me to focus when the previous sections of this book were about creating change in the here and now. It's true that I want to make my surroundings beautiful with as little money as possible. However, I also want to make sure that I am laying a foundation in my home, garden, and future bank account that will ensure that the beauty I create is not just temporary. Like planting seeds that will bear fruit in the seasons to come, sound financial planning today has the capacity to grow into economic security for you and your family in the tomorrows to come.

My concerns about your financial future rest on some assumptions. First I'm not sure if you should count on the availability of Social Security for your retirement. We have all heard about the concerning predictions about the status of this program, which is in large part based on the difficulty inherent in having a declining workforce charged with funding a growing elderly population.

Even if it is available to you, have you considered how much (little!) that benefit amounts to? According to the Social Security Administration, the average monthly benefit for July 2009 was $1,159 for retired workers(U.S. Social Security Administration, 2009, table 1). Would that amount of income pay for your present expenses? Does that amount seem like a lot or adequate for your needs?

Did you know that many Baby Boomers (those born between 1946-1964) currently have less than $200,000 saved for retirement, with few years left to save (Social Security Privatization, March 21, 2005, ¶ 17)? That may seem like a pleasant sum to contemplate, but it is important to consider the practical implications of how far that will actually go. We certainly don't want to get to the point of hoping that we don't live "too long," knowing that our savings will be gone!

Most financial advisors recommend that you withdrawal only four to five percent of your money in any one year to make it last for your lifetime. Five percent of $200,000 is about $833 per month. Add that to the *average* present day Social Security benefit and that equals $1992

This shows the effect of starting saving at 21 by Nan compared to
trying to catch up ten years later by Dan

Nan started at age of 21			Dan started at age of 31		
Year	Contribution	Year end value	Year	Contribution	Year end value
21	$5,000	$5,400	21	$0	$0
22	$5,000	$11,232	22	$0	$0
23	$5,000	$17,531	23	$0	$0
24	$5,000	$24,333	24	$0	$0
25	$5,000	$31,680	25	$0	$0
26	$5,000	$39,614	26	$0	$0
27	$5,000	$48,183	27	$0	$0
28	$5,000	$57,438	28	$0	$0
29	$5,000	$67,433	29	$0	$0
30	$5,000	$78,227	30	$0	$0
31	$0.00	$84,486	31	$5,000	$5,400
32	$0.00	$91,244	32	$5,000	$11,232
33	$0.00	$98,544	33	$5,000	$17,531
34	$0.00	$106,428	34	$5,000	$24,333
35	$0.00	$114,942	35	$5,000	$31,680
36	$0.00	$124,137	36	$5,000	$39,614
37	$0.00	$134,068	37	$5,000	$48,183
38	$0.00	$144,794	38	$5,000	$57,438
39	$0.00	$156,377	39	$5,000	$67,433
40	$0.00	$168,887	40	$5,000	$78,227
41	$0.00	$182,398	41	$5,000	$89,886
42	$0.00	$196,990	42	$5,000	$102,476
43	$0.00	$212,749	43	$5,000	$116,075
44	$0.00	$229,769	44	$5,000	$130,761
45	$0.00	$248,151	45	$5,000	$146,621
46	$0.00	$268,003	46	$5,000	$163,751
47	$0.00	$289,443	47	$5,000	$182,251
48	$0.00	$312,598	48	$5,000	$202,231
49	$0.00	$337,606	49	$5,000	$223,810
50	$0.00	$364,615	50	$5,000	$247,115
51	$0.00	$393,784	51	$5,000	$272,284
52	$0.00	$425,287	52	$5,000	$299,466
53	$0.00	$459,310	53	$5,000	$328,824
54	$0.00	$496,054	54	$5,000	$360,530
55	$0.00	$535,739	55	$5,000	$394,772
56	$0.00	$578,598	56	$5,000	$431,754
57	$0.00	$624,886	57	$5,000	$471,694
58	$0.00	$674,876	58	$5,000	$514,830
59	$0.00	$728,867	59	$5,000	$561,416
60	$0.00	$787,176	60	$5,000	$611,729
61	$0.00	$850,150	61	$5,000	$666,068
62	$0.00	$918,162	62	$5,000	$724,753
63	$0.00	$991,615	63	$5,000	$788,133
64	$0.00	$1,070,944	64	$5,000	$856,584
65	$0.00	$1,156,620	65	$5,000	$930,511
66	$0.00	$1,249,149	66	$5,000	$1,010,352
67	$0.00	$1,349,081	67	$5,000	$1,096,580
68	$0.00	$1,457,008	68	$5,000	$1,189,706
69	$0.00	$1,573,568	69	$5,000	$1,290,283
70	$0.00	$1,699,454	70	$5,000	$1,398,905

The method of calculation is the simplest and is used for order of magnitude. It is the sum of
12 monthly payments times 1.08 which assumes a 8% return

per month in income. Would that pay your present expenses? You won't have the credit cards then, you say? Or the mortgage payment? I hope not, for your sake, kids.

We also need to consider our growing expectation of having nice things. One study found that boomers will not be "satisfied" with a lifestyle during retirement that reflects the modesty of their parents' retirement expectations, and yet most are still not saving enough money for the years ahead (Cruz, 2008, ¶ 5).

As we discuss these realities, my goal is to give you a solid basis from which to understand some of the areas that you need to consider. Financial planning often has an emotional component. By training and vocation, I am an expert in investments, not a therapist. I cannot provide counseling, but I can help you see how growing money can be amazing! Keep in mind, though, that the pages in this book are a mere introduction and no substitute for the sound advice that a financial advisor can provide when addressing your unique needs. I provide an overview of this field, including advice about how to choose the right help for you, in a section below.

Maximize & Economize

The Nan and Dan story is often told in financial institutions because it's easy to relate to and works as a great illustration of the importance of saving now. In this story, Nan and Dan both finish college and look out over the great horizon that is their future.

"Ah," says Dan. "At long last I have a real job with money so that I can finally get the things I've always wanted." Dan spends the next few years collecting the things he has worked hard to finally have: a big truck, stereo system, four-wheeler, etc. He is very happy.

Nan, too, is excited to have a job and make some money, but she spends less than Dan on purchases and instead begins saving for her retirement. Every year, she spends a little less than she makes and saves the difference in a tax-deferred account. (We will talk about all the details further in the chapter.) After ten years, however, Nan stops saving.

Meanwhile Dan has a bit of an epiphany and begins to be concerned that he needs to have something set aside for retirement. So Dan begins to save. He saves the same amount annually that Nan did and continues saving until the year he retires.

Nan only saved for ten years and Dan saved for MANY years, but their piles of money are not equal. Whose savings is larger? This is the really weird part of the story, for Nan's pile of money is actually WAY bigger than Dan's and she only saved for ten years and then STOPPED.

Check out the table, investing starting at 21 to see the benefits of starting early. But don't loose heart, my dears, keep looking! Some of us went back to college later yet or had other reasons not to begin saving for retirement in our 20s or 30s. It is *never* too late; the next chart shows why it remains true that you need to begin now, even if your 20s and 30s are behind you. Nan isn't as well-off as if she'd started at 21, but she's still better off than if she procrastinated yet ten more years (and don't those years pass quickly now that we are older?!)

Now, these days, it seems that college students are graduating older and older, taking longer to get out of school, often because they are concurrently working, trying to pay for classes. So, taking that into account, the following chart shows what happens even if Nan graduated and started saving ten years later, comparing her earnings to Dan who remained tempted by material possessions upon graduation

This shows the effect of starting saving at 31 by Nan compared to trying to catch up ten years later by Dan

	Nan started at age of 31			Dan started at age of 41	
Year	Contribution	Year end value	Year	Contribution	Year end value
31	$5,000	$5,400	31	$0	$0
32	$5,000	$11,232	32	$0	$0
33	$5,000	$17,531	33	$0	$0
34	$5,000	$24,333	34	$0	$0
35	$5,000	$31,680	35	$0	$0
36	$5,000	$39,614	36	$0	$0
37	$5,000	$48,183	37	$0	$0
38	$5,000	$57,438	38	$0	$0
39	$5,000	$67,433	39	$0	$0
40	$5,000	$78,227	40	$0	$0
41	$0.00	$84,486	41	$5,000	$5,400
42	$0.00	$91,244	42	$5,000	$11,232
43	$0.00	$98,544	43	$5,000	$17,531
44	$0.00	$106,428	44	$5,000	$24,333
45	$0.00	$114,942	45	$5,000	$31,680
64	$0.00	$496,054	64	$5,000	$360,530
65	$0.00	$535,739	65	$5,000	$394,772
66	$0.00	$578,598	66	$5,000	$431,754
67	$0.00	$624,886	67	$5,000	$471,694
68	$0.00	$674,876	68	$5,000	$514,830
69	$0.00	$728,867	69	$5,000	$561,416
70	$0.00	$787,176	70	$5,000	$611,729

The method of calculation is the simplest and is used for order of magnitude. It is the sum of 12 monthly payments times 1.08 which assumes a 8% return

This illustration is not a prediction or projection of investment results, does not constitute a solicitation for sale and is for educational purposes only. This information is not meant to be personalized; you should seek the advice of a professional regarding your investments.

These tables are based on some assumptions, but the crazy, awesome fact about compounding is that saving early can make the money grow substantially bigger. This is the reason that I want you to save money on things you buy by using deals and discounts whenever possible. The only money you can use for investments is cash - that's Real Money to me - and to save cash you've got to have cash. Start as soon as possible to save for your future. Please remember that starting today is better than starting next week. Of course it would have been better to have started LAST week, but that's past. Take the perspective that today is next week's last week and start TODAY.

This shows the effect of starting saving at 41 by Nan compared to trying to catch up ten years later by Dan

	Nan started at age of 41			Dan started at age of 51	
Year	Contribution	Year end value	Year	Contribution	Year end value
41	$5,000	$5,400	41	$0	$0
42	$5,000	$11,232	42	$0	$0
43	$5,000	$17,531	43	$0	$0
44	$5,000	$24,333	44	$0	$0
45	$5,000	$31,680	45	$0	$0
46	$5,000	$39,614	46	$0	$0
47	$5,000	$48,183	47	$0	$0
48	$5,000	$57,438	48	$0	$0
49	$5,000	$67,433	49	$0	$0
50	$5,000	$78,227	50	$0	$0
51	$0.00	$84,486	51	$5,000	$5,400
52	$0.00	$91,244	52	$5,000	$11,232
67	$0.00	$289,443	67	$5,000	$182,251
68	$0.00	$312,598	68	$5,000	$202,231
69	$0.00	$337,606	69	$5,000	$223,810
70	$0.00	$364,615	70	$5,000	$247,115

The method of calculation is the simplest and is used for order of magnitude. It is the sum of 12 monthly payments times 1.08 which assumes a 8% return

Though Nan and Dan's piles of money are both quite big and I think you'd agree that either amount would be luscious for a retirement account, remember that Dan contributed a significant amount more of hard-earned Real Money than Nan who made a point to make contributions years earlier. In other words, wise Nan not only had more money for her retirement, she also had more money to spend on paint, gardening supplies, and other items that she could use to live beautifully *before* retirement. However you look at this, no matter what your financial situation today, planning and saving now is far better than putting it off for any amount of time. It is time that simply cannot be bought back!

If you already have a bit of a nest-egg you can use the *Rule of 72* to estimate how quickly your money may double (Bonham, CFA, 2001, p. 574) Divide the compound interest rate by 70 or 72. So if you have $5,000 saved and it is earning 8%, the money will double, according to this simple formula, to $10,000 in nine years (72/ 8 = 9).

Beautify
There is nothing more beautiful than people who recognize their value, are strong and self-sufficient, and take care of themselves so that they maintain their happiness and health throughout their lives. Physical health is an important component of this, as is financial health... and as we well know, the two can be related. In the following pages, I will teach you how to become a beautiful, financially-independent person.

Retirement—Protect Your Head from the Death Rays

This section explains some of the tax implications of retirement accounts. Of course, this is an overview and you should definitely speak to your tax professional for what's best for your situation.

I'll be sad, but not surprised, if this turns out to not be your favorite chapter of the book. You may want to get the aluminum foil out right now and craft a clever chapeau to protect your brain from the death rays. I'm going to explain the following concepts because you need to know them, but I promise to do what I can to bring a bit of quirkiness to the topic. (I wish that I could stick into the book some scratch and sniff sections to make this section really fun, but alas, no can do.) I usually draw pictures for my clients to make certain concepts easier to grasp, and I have created a version of my scribblings in this chapter just for you. Ready?

Picture a circle. Put your retirement plan inside the circle. While the money stays inside the circle it grows without being taxed each year. It is tax-deferred. ALL money invested in retirement plans grow tax-deferred. Tax-deferred growth allows money to grow faster as dividends and interest stay in the account without being taxed each year, allowing a larger base for compounding. That is awesome news because more money is becoming a lovely stash for your future!

The entire process of retirement accounts and investments is overseen by a variety of agencies that make regulations, with the IRS the prime organization. The IRS has an odd communication style that may seem like a foreign language, so let me translate some basic information.

Retirement accounts of ALL kinds have one thing in common. While growing inside the protection of the special retirement account, the investments grow WITHOUT having to pay taxes on any growth, YET. This benefit is called 'tax-deferred growth.' In a tax-deferred account, money can sit and grow for years and years without paying taxes on it. *Pre-tax* retirement savings accounts provide the excellent benefit of lowering your taxable income *in the present year.* If you earn $70,000 and save $10,000 pre-tax, you have removed $10K from your taxable income and are taxed on only $60K. You pay less tax now, which means, of course, that later you will pay taxes on the money placed in the account pre-tax and on the growth.

Yes, you will have to eventually pay, but doing so later rather than now could be a good thing. Why could postponing taxes be good? Well because if you think you will have a lower tax bracket in retirement, when it is time to pay those postponed taxes, the actual amount that you will pay may be lower than taxes you would pay today. Shake yourself and pay attention. You know how awesome it is to save money; saving taxes while saving for your future is even better.

In my brain sometimes pictures work better than just words. If that is also true for you maybe this idea will help. I envision tax-deferred accounts surrounded by a lead wrapper or envelope. While money is in the retirement account, it is inside the protected lead wrapper and can't be taxed. You know, like Superman was powerless to see through lead? You see my reasoning here? It's an exaggerated way to say that the IRS 'can't see' or doesn't tax, that account.

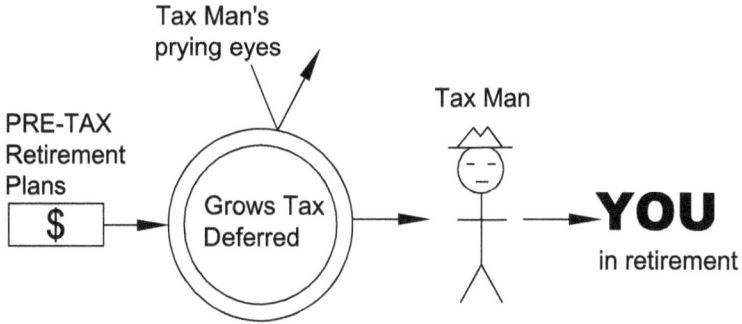

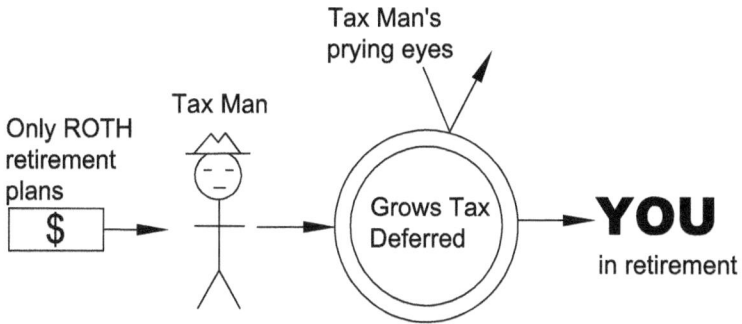

How long can that go on, though? Eventually, the government is going to want to collect all those deferred taxes. Let's drill down one more level for more information.

That tax-deferred benefit has conditions; you knew it would. The tax regulations are used to modify behavior. (I am not going to begin to discuss if it is reasonable for a government to do this or not.) The government believes that retirement savings should be encouraged, so the tax regulations are written to discourage—through the use of penalties and taxes—the early withdrawal of money from a retirement account.

Regulations also ensure that you *do* eventually remove money from out of the lead wrapper so that income can finally be taxed.

You can be any age to open a retirement account as far as the IRS is concerned, though some investment institutions and mutual funds do have age regulations, such as 16, 18 or 21 years of age. In any case, you do have to be earning money to open an account.

Once you contribute money into a retirement account, you can't take it out again until you are at least 59.5 years old. If you do, you will pay taxes *and* penalties. You *can* roll in into similarly titled account at another institution, such as one IRA to another IRA, but you may not withdraw it for use even if you lost your job, if you are losing your house, or if any other catastrophic life event happens. Let me clarify this. It's *your* money, so you *can*, technically, take it. But, regardless of the circumstances, you will pay taxes and penalties if you do so.

Now back to the fun world of tax deferred savings. I've told you when you *can't* take the money. But there is more. You *must* begin taking money from the account, removing it from the lead wrapper so that it can be taxed, after you are 70.5 years old. There are regulated minimum amounts that must be removed from all pre-tax retirement accounts. These withdrawal amounts are called *Required Minimum Distributions* or RMDs.

When you have a pre-tax retirement account, you *must* begin taking RMDs the April after you are 70.5 years old or you will be penalized 50%—half of the amount you *should* have taken out that year.

Retirement accounts all grow tax-deferred but then fall into (as of this writing) two categories: 1) accounts in which money is contributed into a retirement account on what is called a 'pre-tax' basis, and 2) Roth accounts, which are NOT pre-tax retirement accounts. So, money in retirement accounts grows 'tax-deferred,' but the money might or might not have been contributed into the account on a 'pre-tax' basis.

Understanding the pre-tax part is like watching anything be poured through a funnel. If we put your paycheck into this funnel, the initial amount prior to the pour, would be your gross pay. As the money pours through the funnel and is processed various items are removed, including your retirement contribution. (I will not bore you with all the items that are withdrawn, but you can examine your pay stub to see your deductions. Most young people get mad the first time they do this; those of us who are older are more resigned.)

Suffice it to say that taxes are also taken out but know that the contribution to your retirement account has already been removed *before* these taxes. Any money that was removed from your check BEFORE this point is *pre-tax*. All money that is removed *AFTER* this point in the funnel is after-tax.

Why speak in terms of taxes? Because it is primarily taxes and the tax treatment of these accounts that differentiate them. So it may be blinding you, but please slog on!

If you have a retirement plan at work, by the time you receive your check your retirement contribution money has usually been removed from your check before taxes and placed into the tax-deferred retirement account. If you do not participate in a retirement plan at work, or you work for yourself and individually participate in a retirement plan, any money that you may contribute to your retirement account may or may not have been contributed on a pre-tax basis. You should ask your advisor, your accountant, attorney or tax preparer about the status and whether or not you may be able to claim this money when filing your taxes.

Pre-tax retirement accounts have many names (401ks, 403bs, SIMPLE IRAs, SEP IRAs, 457 plans, etc.) and various rules about what kind of entity (company or firm) is eligible to have which kind of retirement account, how much individuals can earn and still contribute, and how much each person can contribute. Pre-tax retirement accounts are almost the only retirement accounts you can get from your employer or on your own.

Regardless of the name or individual differences, these accounts have in common the concept that you can elect to put money into them that will not be taxed until you are of retirement age. You do have to contribute for any of this to matter to you. The studies that continue to pile up demonstrate that most people's paralysis and inaction on retirement savings is growing. If you have a plan at work you elect how much money to put in, though there are maximum amounts allowed by their individual regulations. The accounts are available, through either employers or individual election, to everyone. If you have to set an account up on your own, get help if you are overwhelmed. There are plenty of advisors all over your region to assist you. It is your job simply to PUT MONEY IN HERE! Make contributions. If you are eligible for you firm's plan, participate. Can you hear me?

ROTH Accounts

Since ALL retirement accounts by their very nature allow invested money to grow tax-deferred, the only difference at this level is their tax treatment by the IRS *before* or *after* growth. Roth accounts are after-tax retirement accounts; the benefit of these accounts as compared to pre-tax retirement accounts is that it is never taxed again. Because it is never taxed again, the IRS does not control withdrawals. There are still penalties for taking any money out of the account before age 59 1/2, though the Roth IRA has exceptions for the purchase of a first home and hardship. Please check with an advisor, tax professional, or the IRS for information that is specifically tailored to your situation.

Another advantage of a Roth is that if you'd rather save the money indefinitely, past age 70 1/2, you may. There are penalties for not taking your money, as there are with the other retirement account type, but this account gives you the option to weigh those penalties against the entirety of your financial situation, including your own comfort level. I can imagine myself past my earning years getting even quirkier than I am today. No matter how much money you have saved, it takes faith to relax and not fret about all the things that might go wrong. By that time of your life you will have seen many things go wrong – and right- for friends and family. You will know that the unexpected isn't quite as surprising as you likely thought when you were 20 years old with your adorable bright shiny face looking out on life as your great adventure. Having a pot of money that you can leave untouched, 'just in case,' could give a great deal of comfort.

ROTH IRAs and Roth 401ks are the *only after-tax* retirement accounts. What that means is that you *may not* contribute money into these accounts before taxes. The money will, as in ALL retirement accounts, grow in a tax-deferred account but, because there was no pre-tax benefit, when the money is removed from the retirement account it is NEVER TAXED AGAIN. This is the only account of its kind.

Then why don't more folks have a Roth? For one thing, there are income limits. Also, it may be wise to take advantage first of the pre-tax savings available with every other kind of retirement plan. There is no pre-tax benefit for Roths. If you earn $70,000 and put $10,000 into a Roth account you are still taxed as a person earning $70,000.

You may be able to take advantage of *both* types of retirement accounts; talk with your tax professional. Pre-tax retirement plans have benefits and also have Required Minimum Distributions. After-tax plans have different benefits and no Required Minimum Distributions.

Income Limits and Other Wrappers

I met with a professional early in my practice who had been poor for many years and then as an older adult went to school and became a doctor. He was making more money than he had ever dreamed, but he wanted to be sure that he would have plenty in retirement and never be poor again. He was hoping to allow whatever money he saved to grow without being taxed, but income and retirement plan contributions limits didn't allow him to save the amount of money he need to save for the retirement that he planned. What else could he do?

There aren't many instruments that can solve this problem but there are some. Tax-deferred bonds have been used for years, but annuities also work for this purpose. An annuity is an investment account that allows tax-deferred growth. An annuity benefit is the contractual commitment of the annuity company that, as long as the company remains solvent, they will pay you a certain percentage of your money every year for the rest of your life as a pension. Annuities have costs that are higher than some other investment options so consider them carefully. There are various special features that can be added—for a cost—to an annuity that might address needs or concerns that you have.

Some advisors hate annuities because of the additional costs, and some think they serve a good purpose. The financial services industry uses the term 'suitability' to refer to making the right financial choice. In this case, the 'suitability' of annuities depends on *your needs and situation.* As a financial professional, I show you the options that I believe meet your goals, risk tolerance and tax situation and then I let you decide what is best for your particular situation, revealing all costs as I go. Annuities can be a great choice, and sometimes not so much.

An annuity benefit is the contractual commitment of the annuity company that, as long as the company remains solvent, they will pay you a certain percentage of your money every year for the rest of your life as a pension.

When Will I Pay Taxes on Annuities?

All this tax talk is to give you some basic information. If it isn't your specialty, and it isn't *my* specialty, the entire topic can be confusing. As we learned earlier, tax treatment has to do with pre-tax benefits and tax-deferral. Annuity money may NOT have been contributed pre-tax unless the account is specifically a Traditional IRA (not a Roth IRA). If contributions are made, as in the doctor's case, because the amount of money socked away is greater than the amount that is allowed in traditional retirement plans, the money is contributed AFTER-TAX, so has no pre-tax benefit.

In an annuity, the contributions grow *tax-deferred* and cannot be removed, without penalty and taxes, before age 59 1/2. When you take income out of the account, you will pay tax on the GROWTH only. There are NO Required Minimum Distributions for an unqualified (non-retirement plan) annuity. So you may leave the money in the account as long as you wish. Another reason that annuities may provide a good fit for your needs is their 'bells and whistles.' As pensions have disappeared and downturns in the stock market have shaken Baby Boomers' expectations, annuity companies have filled the void with offers of income guarantees and bonuses on deposits. Check with an advisor to decide if these vehicles are suitable for you.

What Does This Mean?

The more you save, the more you have. Yeah, but you knew that already! Saving is a good thing, and the sooner you do it, the better. However, savings is only part of the plan; it is also important to invest it in a way that safely maximizes your return. Pre and post tax retirement accounts help; Pre-Tax savings lower your present income and may then lower your present taxes. When you *do* pay taxes in the future you think that you will have a lower bracket. If your account is matched through your work place, you could add even more money to your retirement savings. Excellent!

After-Tax retirement savings vehicles will not lower your present income, but they can be held as long as you'd like to save. And they will not be taxed again. Hooray!

Annuities allow larger amounts to be saved and allow special features to your savings, such as increases in the growth of your future income. They may or may not have a pre-tax benefit and can be written to provide an income like a pension.

Quick Tips

- There are two basic retirement accounts, pre tax and after tax. All retirement accounts fall into one of these two categories.

- These accounts are differentiated by their tax treatment.

- Both types of account allow tax-deferred growth.

- There is a pre-tax kind of account, which allows money that you deposit into the account to be removed from your taxable income for that year.

- Pre-tax accounts have stipulations on withdrawal called Required Minimum Distributions.

- There is also a Roth account that has no pre-tax benefit.

- There is no RMD on Roth accounts and distributions are never taxed, neither initial deposit nor growth.

- There are income limits for these accounts.

- Annuities are a hybrid of these types of accounts in which retirement money grows tax-deferred.

- Initial money placed into the account is not ever taxed again, but growth is taxed at distribution.

- Annuities offer, at a cost, guaranteed income for life.

- Check with an expert for the details about retirement accounts. They do matter; you just don't have to know them off the top of your own head.

The point is: SAVE!

. . . .

❧ 13 ❦

When to Use an Advisor - Help!

The financial planning field is very broad. It's like the law or medicine, teaching or construction. There are so many directions or fields within the main subject that one person cannot do all the subjects well and most lean towards one area of specialty. In the case of teachers for example, one may teach college at the graduate level on a very technical topic, while another may work with kindergarten students. Both are teachers, but they work with very different types of students and on very different subjects.

Financial advisors have similar opportunities. As people, they may be big picture types who are closer to economists in viewing the broader economic conditions, or they may be advisors who are also pros at managing your taxes or creating client budgets.

The various designations and terms used for advisors may not make these roles clear. There is a lot of confusion about which type of advisor does what service. Aware of the public's confusion, industry regulations have been put in place to protect consumers and clarify things. Despite that goal, they are not always successful. For instance, you probably don't know that advisors are not permitted to be called an 'advisor' unless they have passed and maintained a certain license.

Based on our capacities, talents, and interests, advisors with similar licenses or designations may choose to specialize in the type of people with whom they prefer to work. Like the teachers above, one who prefers adults and another who prefers little ones, advisors may only work with clients with particular jobs, such as airline pilots or chiropractors, or may specialize in the type of business they like to do, such as retirement planning or stock trading.

Depending on the type of business model the advisor has for her business, she may charge a fee for services, may work on commission, or may combine those two. Additionally, an advisor may be accepting any new client or may only take clients with a certain amount of money to invest. There are pros and cons to both types of advisor. Do research that is appropriate to your individual situation, including letting the advisors with whom you are considering working tell you their reasons. I can't say what's 'right for you' because I haven't spoken with you. But I assure you that there are many qualified individuals who offer worlds of sound financial advice.

Regardless of the licenses or designations, to properly give advice you and your financial professional should discuss roles, compensation, and expectations. You should discuss how decisions are made and have a two-way conversation about your goals and resources, problems or concerns and values and financial outlook. Your risk tolerance and net worth, appropriate financial tools, and plans for reaching your goals should also be discussed. You should have regular evaluations to revisit your financial 'map' and it should be pleasant and feel comfortable.

When do you need an advisor?

Sometimes you just want to make sure that you're on track with what you're doing and with your plans. Many advisors with whom I work, myself included, always offer half an hour for that kind of chat for no fee. Why would we meet with you and give you some general information for nothing? Because we hope that when you have money to invest, when you change jobs, when you get an inheritance, when you win the lottery for Pete's sake, that you'll remember us fondly and come back. We hope that you will have had a good experience with us, have found us honest and helpful and that you send your friends and relatives. Moreover, this way of doing business suits our style: we are good at what we do and we enjoy talking with others about how we can help them.

If that's the kind of info you are looking for, ask around in your town and see who you could meet with. There is no shortage of available professionals. I recommend interviewing people so that you can find the professional who helps you understand *your* money. Sharing the details of how much you earn and your life goals is a very private conversation. It's also some pretty confusing stuff. But trust me. You *can* find a financial advisor who not only does a good job for you, but is a coach, teaching you in simple terms exactly what products and processes are being used, as well as someone with whom you feel comfortable. Remember, too, that you do the best you can but you can't possibly know it all. Convicted tricksters have made the news because they fooled a lot of smart, careful people.

As you are looking around, you may see designations, or even abbreviations based on designations, and want to know what these mean. Licenses, which are regulated by government entities, are not *designations,* which are offered by private entities. Some designations include:

CFP- Certified Financial Planner
ChFC – Chartered Financial Consultant
CLU- Chartered Life Underwriter
CFA- Chartered Financial Analyst
RIA- Registered Investment Advisor

Advisor's have different educational histories, practises and interests. Those advisors that seek designations sometimes do so because they began their practise without much advanced financial education. They want to better prepare themselves for their work. Other advisors, have either advanced financial degrees, like me, or many years of experience and a rich family history of financial service. My friend, Jim Kishbaugh of Danville, Pennsylvania, is such an advisor and has served his clients with integrity and knowledge, as did his father before him.

In your field you probably know many people who have not taken the exact same educational path. Some advisors may have gone to school in another field, changed directions and become an advisor and now they wish to know more.

Before you can ask questions, know what you're looking for, what kind of help you need. Have at least some idea of what types of advisors provide that assistance. What questions should you ask when interviewing advisors? The Security and Exchange Commission (the SEC; for more info see www.SEC.gov) suggest you ask these questions:

What experience do you have, especially with people in my circumstances?

Where did you go to school? What is your recent employment history?

What licenses do you hold? Are you registered with the SEC, a state, or FINRA?

What products and services do you offer?

Can you only recommend a limited number of products or services to me? If so, why?

How are you paid for your services? What is your usual hourly rate, flat fee, or commission?

Have you ever been disciplined by any government regulator for unethical or improper conduct or been sued by a client who was not happy with the work you did?

For registered investment advisers, will you send me a copy of both parts of your Form ADV? (This is a form filed by Register Investment Advisors with the Security and Exchange Commission. According to the SEC the form gives "information about the advisor's education, business and disciplinary history.")

Remember that you're the boss, but your advisor is the experienced coach. That advisor has a job, which is to prepare you for various scenarios, good and bad, and help you navigate to a cozy land where your goals and dreams are realized and where you feel knowledgeable and in control.

• •

I know that you are aware of this, but men and women are different. Why do I bring that up here? Because we deal with money very differently. That fact concerns me because of the consequences of those differences. In the next chapter, we'll see important tips that will help you plan better, both together and with a partner who may have a different way of looking at your joint financial future.

❧ 14 ❧

Boys and Girls
are
Different

Why have an entire section devoted to differences between men and women? Women and men run successful businesses, earn degrees and break down barriers every day. Sure, there are physical and physiological differences between them, but what has any of this to do with money?

The facts are these:
Women live on average five years longer than men (Brown, 2008, ¶ 6). Women earn less for many reasons, and spend less time working in paid positions outside the home. On average women are out of the workplace ten years more than men (Wall & Bahr, n.d., ¶ 6). If women invest in retirement accounts at work, they usually invest too conservatively (Bodnar, 2006, ¶ 5). As a result, substantially more women age 65 or older live in poverty than men (U.S Government Accountability Office [U.S. GAO], October 11, 2007, ¶ 2).

Furthermore, men and women approach money management issues differently, resulting in a lack of communication about essential matters. Consider that 46% of men say that money worries interfere with their relationships and 55% of women agree; however, both partners too often avoid talking about money or developing a financial management plan. Men are less likely to hear their partner's money concerns. When asked if their wife is worried about retirement savings, 46% of men said no. Survey results, however, demonstrated that 67% of their wives had voiced such concerns (Marriage and Money, table 3, 4). Women prefer to make decisions by consensus while men most often are very comfortable making a decisions alone and moving on that decision without discussion (Millan & Piskaldo, 1999, p. 4). Moreover, according to psychologists, men are much more likely to make large purchases without speaking to their partners about it (Millan & Piskaldo, 1999, p. 4). These differences together set the stage for considering the other differences that men and women have when approaching money management.

For Women

The research shows that women want to learn about money as it relates to *life*, not just investment returns. Women want a plan for retirement income, for saving and investing, and for broader issues such as caring for their children and donating to charity. Women don't care about making high returns simply to accumulate wealth. They want money for the things it can help them do with their lives (Jennifer Openshaw, Currents, March 2002, ¶ 2, 3).

Though women manage large budgets for home and business, we frequently have gaps in our own long-term financial knowledge. How much will we need for retirement? Many women don't have a clue as to how much they will need, or they have an unrealistically low figure in mind (Women's Institute for a Secure Retirement [WISER], December 4, 2004, ¶ 4). If we finally DO invest we do so too conservatively, in CD's or savings accounts. We rely on bankers to handle our investments instead of brokers.

One of the most startling examples of this handing over of financial responsibility is the 2007 split of former news anchor Paula Zahn and her husband of twenty-five years. Apparently Zahn had handed over every aspect of her financial control to her husband. This is how *People Magazine* reported the situation:

On Aug. 24, Zahn, 51, filed a civil suit in New York Supreme Court. In it she contends that shortly before marrying Cohen in 1987, she handed her financial affairs over to him; she is now demanding that he provide a detailed account of how he invested portions of her estimated $25 *million in earnings over the last two decades. Alleging that Cohen, 59, had spun 'a Byzantine web' of investments ... Zahn's attorneys say that she is now ready to assume responsibility for her own financial security* (Unhappy Ending, 2007, ¶ 2).

Unfortunately, Zahn is not alone. The author of "*Money: a Memoir*," by Liz Pearle, confesses to having had powerful jobs as a corporate titan, managing large accounts and making bold decisions but not managing her own money or even knowing how to balance her checkbook (Sachs, 2006). I find it hard to comprehend how someone who can read and do basic math can fail to understand how to balance a checkbook, but this example comes up more often than it should.

When women love and trust someone we apparently have no problem releasing control, and foregoing any knowledge - about our finances. Whether this is a partner or a financial advisor, this is YOUR money and you may not abdicate *total* responsibility for it. You simply may not. Learn what you need to know about life insurance, annuities and the fun of compound interest and plan for your future!

And there's more about women: only 41 percent of women participate in the 401(k) at work and only 15 percent of women who live with someone feel responsible for their retirement planning (Williams, ¶ 3). We want someone else to "take care of us," even with our advanced degrees and CEO positions. Know this, ladies and gentlemen: When it comes to retirement savings, it is estimated that you will need 126% of your present income in retirement to have the same lifestyle. This takes into account inflation, life span and medical expenses (Associated Press, July 1, 2008, ¶ 2). There are an awful lot of us who haven't saved enough; that is why more than half of all single women over age 75 are living in poverty (Kostrunek, 2005, p. 16).

Author Anne Letterese wrote,
"Baby boomers, ages 35-50, had the most cosmetic surgery in 1999 with 43% of 4.6 million procedures. Women had 89% of these surgeries (that's 1,760,420 procedures at an average, $2,500 per operation). What is it going to take for us to wake up and spend the same amount of time and money on our futures [as we do in] our mirrors and [with our' spinning classes? Americans spend $300 million on clothes EVERY DAY! C'mon, ladies! Let's get our act together... Don't send or drop off

another flower or greeting card to any woman over 35 until you hug her, look her in the eyes, and say, "Let me see your retirement plan!" (Letterese, 2002, ¶ 9, 13).

Since nine out of ten women will be solely responsible for their own finances at some point in their lives, what happens to women who don't realize their need to plan? Over 75 percent of women are widowed, at an average age of 56, and one in four are broke within two months (Williams, ¶ 2, 3). Frighteningly, a survey of financial advisors found that well over two-thirds of advisors said that men are not planning well for their spouse's well-being after the husband's death. (Koco, May 8, 2006, ¶ 7). Mamma Mia!

Women's average life expectancy is 80, and men's is 75 according to the US Administration on Aging (Brown, 2008, ¶ 6). Women tend to marry older men, (U.S. Census 2000, n.d.) which means that seven out of ten women are expected to outlive their husbands (Administration on Aging, 2000, ¶ 5). And that doesn't even take into consideration the nation's rate of divorce. Assets may be fairly distributed during a divorce settlement but, if the numbers about women and their professional earnings are correct, women may have financial difficulty for years after a split (Stearn, 2006).

Women earn less than men, but we are not earning less because we are less qualified. We earn less in part because of ongoing discrimination, but our diminished earnings are also based on the fact that we make life choices that take us out of the workplace for more time than do men. For example, several countries have recently held discussions about their concerns about a shortage of practicing physicians (Arnst, 2008, ¶ 1). Women, who comprise 49% of medical school enrollments (Nowlan, 2006, ¶ 4), are choosing to work 20 to 25% less than their male counterparts, or completely pull out of the work place entirely to raise children, care for elders and to be home with teens during crucial adolescent years (Arnst, ¶ 2, 5). The areas of practice that women choose to follow in medicine, if they continue to practice at all, are ones in which pay is significantly less than other fields (Arnst, ¶ 7). These choices are occurring in other professions too, with the end result that women are working less and choosing less prosperous areas of practice.

Our financial futures are then compromised further when we make overly conservative decisions about investing. These decisions too often assess so little risk that we face serious consequences from inflation because we are putting money into investments that grow more slowly than costs expand in the economy (B Net, November 1, 2001).

Though the pursuit of money may not be the goal of your life, you *must* take extra care in retirement planning to compensate for your unique situation and your life decisions. Women should carefully consider these important financial factors:

Longevity and reduced earnings may mean you have to live longer with less.

A conservative savings style may not get you to your financial goal.

Evaluate your laissez-faire attitude about retirement planning.

Have a hands-on policy in financial management, whether you work with a professional or on your own.

For Men

What about men? Men more often recognize the importance of retirement savings, begin earlier and apply more resources to the goal.

However, men take risks, erring on the other side of the coin as the low-risk mistakes made by women, and often invest without advice. In surveys, 74% of men find investing fun (Study: Gender Influences Investing Style, 2006, ¶ 6). This may be because of some interesting science. The San Francisco Chronicle reported the results of brain scans that demonstrate that the same section of the male brain that has activity when taking financial risk also lights up when shown "erotic" pictures (Borenstein, 2008, ¶ 1, 2).

So, not only do men really like investing because of how their brains relate to the information, but the biology of men's eyes may help them appreciate the ups and downs of investing. A study found that men have more "M receptors" than women. This causes men to notice an investment's up and down motion because men are more likely to notice movement. Women have "P cones," which cause them to be more likely to notice the characteristics of a thing rather than its motion ("Study Shows Men Invest Differently Than Women," 2008, ¶ 5).

It is interesting, then, that many more women than men report being good investors. Male investors report greed, impatience and overconfidence as the emotions that direct them in their investments (Merrill Lynch, 2005, ¶ 10, 18), which may be why men who use financial advisors report a much higher level of satisfaction and success (Merrill Lynch, 2005, ¶ 19).

However, when men do well with an investment they tend to believe it was because of their own cleverness, and when things do poorly they blame their financial advisor. On the other hand, women believe they do well because of help from an advisor and if they do poorly, it was because of their own mistakes (Millan & Piskaldo, 1999, p. 4).

Financial factors for men:
> Include your partner in financial discussions about both spending and saving.
> Recognize that more balanced results may be achieved with a financial partner.
> Retirement planning must keep your surviving spouse in mind.

The Numbers

ING, a global financial services company, commissioned a survey, called the Retirement Number Survey, to uncover the numbers that are important to people. They found that the numbers folks care about are their own birthdays, or the birthdays of loved ones. That makes sense. Since the survey is titled the "Retirement Number" survey, you may be wondering what else they found (ING, 2008, p. 1).

Part of the survey found that people *want* to understand retirement numbers. They *think* about their retirement, at least sometimes. But the survey also revealed that people find thinking about retirement really *boring* and have no idea how or where to start in figuring out what they might need for retirement. Almost half of survey respondents said they don't like to think about all that confusing stuff at all.

Here's a number that alarmed me. Only 5% of those surveyed consider the amount of their retirement nest egg important. Why isn't this particular number important? Do you think you won't need a retirement nest egg because you know that you'll be winning the lottery, or because Mommy and Daddy are leaving you millions of dollars? Even if that will be your future, surely you have heard of those with windfalls who are now living in poverty.

Maybe you think Social Security will provide you with a great big monthly check? Hear me yelling now as I say, "I hope you like dog food 'cause that's what you are going to be eating if you don't get your butt in gear!"

Amount of monthly contributions for a given number of years to obtain approximately $1,000,000, based on 8% return

Number of years	Monthly contribution	Number of years	Monthly contribution
40	$300	22	$1,395
38	$351	20	$1,690
36	$415	18	$2,065
34	$487	16	$2,550
32	$580	14	$3,190
30	$685	12	$4,075
28	$810	10	$5,350
26	$967	8	$7,300
24	$1,160	6	$10,550

This illustration is not a prediction or projection of investment results, does not constitute a solicitation for sale and is for educational purposes only. This information is not meant to be personalized; you should seek the advice of a professional regarding your investments.

I think I know a number you'd like. If you were the dragon in the fairy tale sitting on a giant pile of gold coins and jewels in a secret cave, I bet you'd like the number that was the total value of that treasure. Think of yourself as the keeper of a treasure as you look at the growing pile of money in your tax-deferred account and retirement planning becomes less boring. I think that you might find a worry free retirement anything BUT boring! Imagine all you could give to charity and to your children and grandchildren.

What You Need to Know

First, estimate an annual income you'll need in retirement. How much are you living on now? Are you content with that level of income? Will you require less or more in retirement? Will your mortgage be paid off? What about costs of healthcare and travel? What do you think will happen over the next 20, 30, 40 or 50 years when you consider inflation? Inflation is the change in the cost of goods or services over time. For instance, how much did candy cost when you were a little kid compared to how much that same candy costs today? My husband always remembers how much a gallon of gas was when he first got his driver's license, and compares that to what gas costs today. The change in price is in part due to inflation.

Second, you need to understand how much you can withdraw each year from the money that you saved. It is generally thought that only about 4% to 5% of the total should be taken per year from your retirement savings account if you want the assets to last throughout your lifetime. Annuities that promise by contract to pay the owner an income for their lifetime usually say that a 4.5-5% annual payout from your total account is the amount you may withdraw if you begin withdrawing money between ages age 45- 74 (depending on the company).

What does that mean to you? If you have $1,000,000 saved, 5% would equal $50,000 per year. If you have half of that saved, withdrawing 5% would provide an annual income of $25,000. If you are the average Baby Boomer cited above who has $200,000 saved for retirement, a withdrawal rate of 5% would mean you would have $10,000 dollars per year, or $833 dollars per month, before paying taxes.

The third step is to figure out how much you will need to save in order to achieve your desired income. If you only withdraw 5% of the total for your annual income, you can multiply the desired income by a factor of 20 to get the total assets needed. For example, if I want a $35,000 annual income multiply $35,000 x 20 = $700,000. This is the amount you'd need to save to have at least that income. If you want an $80,000 income per year, you'd need to save $1,600,000. If you desire $500,000 in annual income, aim for $10,000,000 in total savings.

I am using $1 million for easy figuring, but how much do you have to save to get to $1,000,000? See the table entitled *Amount of Monthly Contibutions for a Given Number of Years to Obtain $1,000,000.*

Using the table you see that you would need to save $300 per month at 8% to have one million dollars in 40 years. If you have 18 years until retirement and you want one million dollars, you need to save $2,065 per month. (No one knows how much money will earn in any given year, or in any ten-year period. We can only use history to see patterns of good times and bad and evaluate average investment returns. Estimates are made in a range, from 7% - 10%, with some figures *including* inflation, and some removing the effects of inflation. By the way, inflation in simple terms, is the change in the cost of candy, or other goods or services, from the price you paid as a child compared to today's price for the same candy, or gallon of gas of pair of jeans.)

Investments in Retirement Accounts – What Is This Money Invested In?

I have referred several times to the return rate, such as citing 8% in the number above. How do you make sure that the savings that you do create get such a return?

Remember the tax-deferred "lead wrapper" and the pre-tax (Required Minimum Distribution-types) or Roth accounts? Both have income limits and contribution limits, so you may also invest in annuities and tax-free savings programs such as bonds.

If you open a retirement account at the bank and a customer service person helps you, the money that you put into the account might go into a CD or a savings account. A CD, or Certificate of Deposit, is a vehicle in which the financial institution guarantees a rate of interest usually partly based on the length of time that the money will be in the CD. The rate will be low but certain. One of the biggest risks to your savings in an account of this type is *inflation risk*, when the price of goods and services grows faster than your money.

If the customer service person brings in a licensed securities' person, or if you use a financial advisor, the retirement account will probably have contributions invested in stocks or bonds or mutual funds. Individuals who have a securities license are registered representatives, or stockbrokers. They work at banks and firms all over town and speak to you about investments in the "stock market." Investments in individual stocks, bonds, or mutual funds have consistently performed at a higher rate of return than CDs over the long term.

Since the 1800s, diversified holdings of stocks have consistently produced a 7% rate of return *after inflation.* With all the wars, shortages, depressions and crises over time, and with the ups and downs of the market, stock performance averages remain relatively stable. Bonds returns are lower; since 1926, their real return, after inflation, has averaged 2.2% based on the research of Jeremy Segal as published in his book *Stocks for the Long Run.*

Most investors don't invest in individual stocks and bonds but use portfolios of several stocks or bonds, or portfolios of a mix of stocks and bonds. These portfolios are mutual funds. They are managed by professional fund managers, some of whom are very good at what they do, and some who are not so good. Therefore, some of these funds perform better than others.

Some authors advise readers about the type of investment they should make. I think that is unwise; you and your adviser should make the best decision for you. It is odd when new clients come to my office and follow the words of a book author religiously. They tell me that they 'should' be invested in growth mutual funds because that's what the author told them was appropriate for them. It isn't possible that I, or any other author, can know your best investment choice. Your investment choices are made based on your goals, your risk tolerance and what you feel comfortable investing in for your time horizon. Blanket statements on what you should be doing aren't accurate.

Additionally, there are "growth" and "income" types of mutual funds. I have had clients come to my office, with a finance book griped firmly in their hand, and insist that I let them invest in "*the* growth fund." There isn't one mutual fund called GROWTH; it's a type of fund, like a carrot is a type of vegetable.

Growth and income mutual funds usually hold a mix of dividend or income-producing stocks or bonds, in addition to stocks of companies that might experience growth to attempt to give the investor a balance. Income mutual funds are those in which the professional managers have chosen stocks or bonds for their income-producing potential. These investments may be invested in government bonds, mortgage securities, junk bonds or stocks that pay dividends. Investors may choose a mutual fund that focuses on growth due to new technologies, the potential for expansion, or above-average earnings potential. These may expose the investor to higher risk than other investment choices.

There are fees associated with mutual funds that include trading costs, commissions and advertising. Reallocation of funds has no additional fee if you are trading funds within one fund company, also called a fund family. You can move funds around whenever you'd like. (Some fund families may restrict frequent trading with additional fees so you should check with your mutual fund.)

Mutual funds offer discounts, or breakpoints, to investors who have hit certain levels of accumulated assets. This breakpoint applies jointly to you and to your spouse's accounts. Breakpoints mean lower costs to both of you in all your accounts and typically occur at $50,000 and $100,000 and then again at $250,000 and above.

These discounts and fees will be different for each fund family and the plan that you have at work may have a totally different fee structure. There are financial experts who despise mutual funds. They prefer groups of investments that act as one's own mutual fund, with stocks and bonds in a portfolio that is diversified and isn't one large holding of a single company's stock.

I have always liked mutual funds as way of making small amounts of money go to work immediately. You should understand that finance is like a lot of things in life; there are many opinions on good ways to do things and there is more than one correct approach.

• •

∾ 15 ∽

So, What's It All About, Alfie?*

So what's it all about, Alfie? There are some basic truths about money. Everyone has a finite amount of dollars and many needs and desires for those funds. I'm sure you've heard news stories about movie stars and sports heroes who were paid enormous sums of money but are now broke. So though you may not have a lot, or may wish you had more, you really need to learn to live with what you have.

You need to be wise. Becoming wise is a process, which really only happens as you move *forward,* sometimes making mistakes and some-times succeeding brilliantly. But to move forward not as smart today as you may be in the future you also have to be bold. Sure, you can mope around, waiting for a magical tomorrow, but happiness and peace and beauty probably won't be hand-delivered to you or drop through the ceiling. You need to *do something* about your situation. Fish or cut bait, baby.

* Lyrics from the song Alfie written by Joss Stone

Where to start? First, please *start.* Start anywhere. Start small. But please just start! Save $20 a day, or a week, or a month. De-clutter the garage, the hall closet, the bathroom medicine cabinet. Use baby steps to develop some momentum and experience. Confidence will begin to well up in your adorable little heart as you move forward towards a brighter, tidier, more prosperous future and others will ask you how you did it. It will take you by surprise when the time comes that you've become the resident expert, believe me. And then you'll look around, take stock of the various areas in your life, and know that you really are living beautifully, in all of the areas that statement implies.

Please do not set yourself up for failure by tackling the biggest job first. Do the boring little jobs first and treat yourself to the job you are most excited about after you have a bit more knowledge and experience and can tackle it wisely, or at least more wisely than without the previous experience. When I painted that three-story house and Mort wisely told me that starting on the back wall was really the best way to go, I nearly cried I was so disappointed. I really wanted the satisfaction of painting the front first! I wanted to see how beautiful the house would look with the lovely creamy paint that we'd chosen. I was mad, too, because I knew he was right. I didn't want to paint the back even in my very enthusiastic state. Obviously he was right and there was little chance that I'd paint it all if it had to be done at the end of the project. That part of the job was going to be boring and not very satisfying.

But, boy, was I proud of myself when it was done! You can use this lesson to recognize the psychology of all of your projects, whether they are the accomplishments of home improvement, garden beautification, or financial stability. Figure out what motivates you and be wise about helping yourself reach your goals. You probably want a lovely retirement and not years filled with worry. *But* you may also want to buy stuff *now.* Maybe you give in to the latter desires more than the boring old retirement. Fix that deficiency, yes, deficiency, by making contributions automatically. Make an effort at thinking about your retirement years in real terms and not as some distant land where things will somehow magically work out, even though you're in debt up to your teeth and you are on your crazy way to lunacy-ville.

Do you really want to fix the kitchen? That could be a big project especially if you are considering a complete redo. I'm all for tackling this project, but think it through. Is this the first job you've ever done on the home improvement journey? Maybe you could work your way from 0 to 60 in the slow lane.

Perhaps you could break the project down into all the many parts and tackle the tasks that require less skill first. Start by painting the walls and see what effect that has on the mood of the room. Another baby-step, if you will, could be picking out and installing new hardware for the cabinets and drawers. If you are tackling this project in smaller, bite-size bits, you might splurge on high-end pulls and knobs. Soak those changes in and see how it all feels before moving ahead.

Do the same with your garden and your finances. Start, do something, invest some money, make an appointment with an advisor or a landscape architect. You don't have to spend a lot but you do have to be smart and creative. Work that creative muscle! I can't tell you exactly how to proceed, but I strongly advise that you remember what we've discussed: envision the future you desire and take steps to get there. With home improvement, that may mean collecting magazines and figuring out what you love about the kitchens and the particular elements that make you feel happy. Is it the color, the window seat, the fabric, the flooring? Is it several elements? With the garden it will be similar; developing a visual picture of what you want to see and moving toward that idea. Financial planning can be both more fun and more complicated, but the basic principles apply: imagine what you want, then get specific in determining the steps that you need to get there. What simple changes, what small steps, can you take to get closer to that vision? Take those steps. Work with a financial advisor. Keep your early efforts small and focused to get results, to actually finish the project.

Did you come out of the womb understanding advanced calculus? Probably not, but you eventually got to a higher level of knowledge by building brick by brick on basic information with each new step or project. Now, look at you. You're pretty darn capable, right?

You can actually be mediocre at many jobs and still do wonderful things; *simple* things, but wonderful things, nevertheless. Whatever steps you are taking, please use cash wisely. Look for opportunities. Move forward in your efforts but balance that with patience. Learn from mistakes and do not beat yourself up, please; just keep puttering around. Don't take things so seriously. Just try it. You can continue to want to be better at the tasks, so long as you recognize that you will not become more capable unless you do them, or variations, over and over.

And in the end, your efforts will be worth it. Your home, garden and financial future will be peaceful and beautiful. Maybe they won't be perfect or regal in scale, but things will be far better because of your efforts than if you had done nothing to advance your dreams. You will be satisfied and happy with your world and with yourself.

Oh, the stories we'll tell of our great adventures.

• •

❧ 16 ❧

Appendix - Yard Sales, Estate Sales & Auctions

Yard Sales — "One man's junk is another man's treasure."
– Anonymous

Why buy stuff used? Won't it be icky? Hasn't a relative ever given you a piece of furniture so you'd have something to sit on instead of plastic crates? Mort and I have found resale shops, auctions and yard sales to be a great way to recycle, save money and have options for our house. One of the great things about yard or garage sales is how far they can help you stretch a dollar. Once you have bought a refrigerator for $5, paying $1000 for a chair at a furniture store really difficult, even if you have the money!

Buying things at full price is using 'Real Money." Real Money has to be used for retirement planning, paying the electric bill, and buying groceries. You can't trade or barter in those instances, you have to use greenbacks. With so many 'pulls' on my cash, I am very careful with it; I try not to use Real Money when a bargain is much better!

The usefulness of certain found items may be readily apparent; it requires some creativity to recognize the possibilities in others. You can develop your creative "muscle" with a bit of effort. It doesn't take imagination or creativity to buy matching selections from a catalog, but it's much more expensive than hunting for a similar item in a flea market or at a yard sale—and not nearly as much fun!

I love that every found item has a story. Mort and I have incorporated items with "pasts" into our lives; they are now serving renewed purposes. Once you repurpose something from a yard sale, you will be amazed at how darn proud of yourself you become. You develop a sense of possibility, pride and almost daring that seems much stronger than you might think. "What the heck," you say to yourself and your partner, hands on your hips and chest puffed out, "Let's try another project!"

A yard sale isn't a store, so there will only be one of the item you're shopping for and if it's reasonably priced and in good shape, you won't be the only very interested buyer. Your goal is to get to that item first! It also helps to have a general idea of what you're looking for, so that you'll know "it" when you find it.

Have realistic expectations and remember, a yard sale is not a custom store where craftspeople are waiting to take your order for the perfect piece for your family. One generally finds solid pieces of furniture in many styles, from reproduction antiques to basic streamlined shapes. These pieces are ripe for keeping as is, or they can be painted black or white for a modern take on classic shapes.

When considering which yard sales to visit notice ads that list 'baby clothes' or 'kid's toys.' What are the chances that this young family will have extra furniture for sale that you would want to add to your home? Frequently these sales feature the cheap mugs or free gifts that one gets from renewing a magazine subscription. But if you are in the market for inexpensive stuff for kids these sales are obviously goldmines!

If you're looking for furniture, seek out yard sales by older couples downsizing or people moving (remember the average family moves every five years). These sales often offer all kinds of house wares, too: bowls, microwave and toaster ovens, flatware, linens, pet accessories, camping items and garden gear like lawn mowers, snow blowers and shovels.

Prices at such sales are generally reasonable as these folks have a good appreciation of the real resale value of things. At homes where folks are selling things because they "bit off more than they could chew" financially and need to reduce debt, the prices are typically too high. They are trying to recoup what they still owe on the furniture.

Some of our coolest items have been bought at yard sales where folks have recently completed additions on their houses. Check ads for phrases like "building materials" and you might find molding, sinks, plywood and windows, all new and at great prices.

Mort and I take Saturdays for our yard sale adventures; we enjoy the cheap fun of spending time together, splitting a bagel and dreaming of hidden treasure. We have found that we get the most out of our excursions by being organized, so we make a map. On Friday night, we look through the sales listed for the weekend. (In the warm months, sometimes the number of yard sales ads that feature interesting key words can freak us out—we don't want to miss any "good stuff!") We print out the list of sales and circle the ones of interest, then number the list of the sales we want to try to make. Then we print out a computer-generated map. We then place numbers on the areas of the map that represent the yard sales, (corresponding to the same number that we mark in the newspaper's list of yard sales) noticing any patterns in the location of the week's yard sales. What section of town are they in? Is this section of town a hotbed of great bargains? (If you are searching for flatware because your forks have all gone missing, it may not matter where you 'shop. But for larger pieces of furniture, you will probably have better success in middle class, and better, sections of town. On the other hand, we have gotten solid mahogany dining tables in really good condition for unbelievable bargains in parts of town that weren't the "good" sections, so location isn't always everything!)

A Word on Yard Sale Etiquette

Mort and I decided early on that we would follow the etiquette of yard sales; we are not in this for the stuff alone, but to spend time together and to furnish the house cheaply and well.

We are early risers and usually get up in time to be the first arrivals at most places. We never do what the professionals do, which is to go the house days before a sale and try to buy the best finds before the sale even begins. Getting to the sale early is the key to getting the items you'd like, but knocking on doors before a sale is an etiquette no-no.

Take cash—small bills and change. You want to get in and out and go to the next sale quickly. Correct change is also helpful for the seller.

Don't be pushy. You DO need to be assertive as this is first-come-first-served shopping, but be polite. You can bargain and bicker over prices, but remember that you're a guest. Treat others as you would want to be treated!

Be respectful of parking. It gets pretty crowded in a neighborhood during yard sales. Watch for people crossing the street and be careful to respect property. Don't walk through the garden or go where you haven't been invited.

Be prompt if you have to come back to pick up large items with a truck or more friends. Leave your number, pay up front and return quickly, unless other arrangements have been made.

Quick Tips
- Have a list of needs/wants/ dreams!

- Be flexible.

- Older sections of town may provide great bargains.

Estate Sales and the Recycling Center

Fifty years ago people didn't have access to the inexpensively made furniture and house wares that we have today. Unless they were wealthy, they passed down the furniture that they had, buying very few pieces new.

Now one only needs to turn on the TV shows about consuming to realize that we have access to a lot of inexpensively made items. That's good, because we can buy new furniture when our moods or fashion trends change, but what are we supposed to do with the perfectly good furniture that we no longer want or need?

That's where our excellent recycling center has been a boon to Mort and me! Our town has made recycling easy and fun for residents by providing a covered garage-size building where folks can place items they no longer need. Sometimes the stuff is damaged, of course, but sometimes it's treasure! We have found exercise equipment, weights, leather pants, a pine corner bookshelf, dressers for the lake house, chairs, magazines, and all kinds of items. Some local towns even have a resale shop at the recycling center and sell things at hugely discounted prices.

Estate Sales

Estate sales usually involve the contents of houses being sold to liquidate a family's assets. They are not always held at the home from which the items are being liquidated, but that has been our experience, and it can make these events seem sad. You bring your own bags, packing material and boxes. (It doesn't hurt to fill the car with whatever you might need.) A line forms outside the house and, at the time listed in the ad or notice, the doors are opened. The object is to grab what you truly think you want and then pay for it when you leave.

When the sale begins and there is a large group waiting to enter the house, only a certain number of people at a time are allowed in. The closer that you are to the front of the line the better your chances for the best pickings. As people buy things and pay for their purchases, another group is allowed in.

This is the ultimate in impulse buying. If you think you truly want this item, you must grab it, or take the tag from it if it is a larger piece such as dresser. Don't take a tag if you are probably NOT interested as the seller has a business to run and you may hurt his or her best chance for a sale by taking a tag from an item you have no intention of buying. You can reconsider, but replace items or tags quickly when you decide NOT to purchase them so others have a chance to buy.

Auctions

An auction is like an estate sale in that there are a large amount of items in one location. The difference is that each item is featured and sold one at a time while buyers are sitting. An auction has a much more relaxed atmosphere, so you have a little more time to consider your options. You may find auction information in newspaper advertisements or auctioneers' direct mailings.

Auctions also provide the opportunity to closely examine each item and ask the seller questions about its history or 'provenance.' You can plug in TVs or other appliances and test their condition. This time to check things out more closely is called the "preview;" previews may occur the day before the auction scheduled and/or in the few hours before the auction begins.

Items for sale are given descriptions and 'lot numbers' for tracking purposes. Generally, finer quality antiques or other items are intermixed with 'box lots' of books, magazines, kitchen wares, dishes or linens. Everyday furniture may also be available and could be sold in between high-end items. And the deals! I've seen leather wingback chairs in almost new condition sell for $200 each and 6-foot tall bookcases for $40!

Auctions can last six hours or more. Refreshments are often available for sale on-site to keep the crowds from leaving, but you can usually bring your own food. High-end items are generally sold earlier in the day before folks get bored and leave. "Bottom feeders" who are looking for bargains, camp furniture or box lots tend to be rewarded for their patience as these items sell very near the end of the day.

To purchase items at an auction you must register before you bid, so bring identification such as a picture ID and a credit card. You will be issued a bidder number, generally on a piece of cardstock so that you can keep track of items that you might like to bid on and tally your purchases. A tab is kept registering what you have won during the bidding.

Payment is usually credit card or cash. Some sellers will accept checks. Be sure what type of payment will be accepted before you bid.

Auctioneers do not talk in funny styles; at least no one ever has at the auctions that we have attended. The auctioneer initially suggests bidding increments, but you may see bidders stating their own bid amounts. Auctioneers typically suggest reasonable bid amounts, so the price of the item will good but generally within an expected price range.

Once you win an item it may be left with you, delivered by a "runner," or kept behind the scenes. Make sure that if your item is kept in the back it is not accidentally removed by other bidders as they exit. These things sometimes occur. Check items before you pay to ensure that you have what you purchased. If you need assistance please ask an auction worker; remember, they may not be professional antique dealers with a lot of knowledge of items or prices. The auction isn't set up like a store with multiple aisles and experienced cashiers. It could take some time to collect your items, check out and get things to your car so be patient and cheerful.

Offer to tip auction workers who help you carry items to your car.

• •

☙ 17 ❧

Glossary

IRA- The name for Individual Retirement Accounts, which may be provided by employers or individuals and whose assets grow tax-deferred. There are many types of IRAs: SEP, SIMPLE, Traditional, Roth and Self-Directed. Withdrawal rules are very similar except for Roth IRAs.

Roth IRA- An Individual Retirement Account that provides tax-deferred growth. Unlike any other retirement account, contributions made to a Roth are not tax deductible. Withdrawals are generally tax-free, but not always. (Such as if the account has been opened less than five years or account owner is less than 59.5 years-old.)

Traditional IRA- See IRA

Annuity- An annuity is a contract offered through insurance companies and useful as part of a retirement strategy. Annuities come in many forms, fixed and variable, and are often used provide steady income in retirement.

Real Money – Paying full price for an item.

Tax-deferred- Indicates the postponing of tax payments. The term is usually used for retirement accounts, but may also include Health Savings Accounts and other accounts. It indicates that the account is not taxed each year as is the case for accounts that are *not* tax-deferred. Taxes may be due prior to deposit (as with Roth IRAs) or may be due upon withdrawal (in the case of other retirement accounts.)

Required Minimum Distribution- According to the IRS, "Required Minimum Distributions (RMDs) generally are minimum amounts that a retirement plan account owner must withdraw annually starting with the year that he or she reaches 70 ½ years of age or, if later, the year in which he or she retires. However, if the retirement plan account is an IRA or the account owner is a 5% owner of the business sponsoring the retirement plan, the RMDs must begin once the account holder is age 70 ½, regardless of whether he or she is retired."

Suitability- The assessment made by a financial advisor after considering a client's risk tolerance, goals and objectives, financial status, needs and holdings.

SIMPLE IRA – see IRA

SEP IRA – see IRA

401(k) – A tax-deferred retirement plan used for businesses. Employers sometimes choose to match employee contributions.

403(b) – A tax-deferred retirement plan used for non-profits, schools and hospitals.

Mutual Fund- An investment that allows investors to own a group of company stocks, bonds or a mix of both. It may also hold government, municipal or corporate bonds.

Stock- Buying stock allows the purchaser to become an owner, in part or whole, of a company. The holder becomes a stockholder in the firm or business. A stock is also called equity. Stocks can be in small or large, domestic or international companies.

Bond- A bond is a debt obligation of a company, government or municipality. Your investment is a loan to the bond issuer and in turn you may receive principal plus interest. A bond is a security and as such has various degrees of risk.

Tax-deferred - Generall refers to an account in which investments compound and taxes are not paid while they remain in the account.

Pre-tax - Typically refers to retirement accounts that allows investments to be deposited into an account prior to taxation.

Inflation Risk - The change in value, from year to year, of goods and services. Inflation rates generally average about three percent per year. Some categories grow at a much steeper rate than others, such as college tuition and health care.

• •

References

5 ridiculously simple health boosters...that have nothing to do with diet or exercise (August 2008, August). *Glamour*, 81.

About.com (2007). *The Cost of Clutter*. Retrieved May 12, 2009, from http://stress.about.com/od/lowstresslifestyle/a/clutter.htm

Administration on Aging (2000). *Older Women*. Retrieved May 18, 2009, from http://www.aoa.gov/naic/may2000/factsheets/olderwomen.html

Alfano, H. (2008). Census Eliminates Home Improvement Survey. *Remodleing Magazine*, (), . Retrieved . Retrieved from http://www.remodeling.hw.net/remodeling-market-data/census-eliminates-key-home-improvement-survey.aspx

Arbor Day Foundation (n.d.). *The Benefits of Trees*. Retrieved May 18, 2009, from http://www.arborday.org/trees/benefits.cfm

Arnst, C. (2008, April 17). Are There Too Many Women Doctors?. *Business Week*.

Associated Press (July 1, 2008). *Women Saving Less than Men for Retirement*. Retrieved May 18, 2009, from http://today.msnbc.msn.com/id/25480689

B Net (November 1, 2001). *Investing with Care- "Women and Investing" Part 1*. Retrieved March 20, 2009, from http://findarticles.com/p/articles/mi_m4021/is_2001_Nov_1/ai_79501188

Bailly, J. (2008, February 15). Get Happy. *Allure*, 194-197.

Bankrate.com (2007). *Gender Spender: Sex Sets Your Money NDA*. Retrieved April 23, 2009, from http://www.bankrate.com/brm/news/sav/20000620a3.asp?caret=2

Bodnar, J. (2006). Money: Women Vs. Men. *Kiplinger*(December 7). Retrieved from http://www.kiplinger.com/features/archives/2006/12/women.html

Bonham, H. B., CFA (2001). *The Complete Investment and Finance Dictionary*. Avon, MA: Adams Media Corporation.

Borenstein, S. (2008, April 5). When the pretty women smiles, men more
    likely to spend freely. *The San Francisco Chronicle*. Retrieved
    from http://www.sfgate.com/cgi-bin/article.cgi?f=/c/a/2008/04/05/
    BUUR10091G.DTL

Bradford, S. L. (2008). The Five Mistakes Married Women Make. *Smart
    Money*. Retrieved from http://www.smartmoney.com/divorce/mar-
    riage/index.cfm?story=mistakes2005

Brown, D. (2008, June 12). Life Expectancy Hits Record High in United States.
    Washington Post. Retrieved from http://www.washingtonpost.com/
    wp-dyn/content/article/2008/06/11/AR2008061101570.html

Brown, D. (2008, June 12). Life Expectancy Hits Record High in the United
    States. *The Washington Post*. Retrieved from http://www.washington-
    post.com/wp-dyn/content/article/2008/06/11/AR2008061101570.html

Brown, M., Ph.D. (2006). When Your Body gets the Blues, Dr. Marie-Annette
    Brown Answers Your Questions [Online exclusive]. . Retrieved April
    21, 2009, from http://www.thebodyblues.com/questionsandanswers.
    html

Byron, E. (2009, February 3). Is the Smell of Moroccan Bazaar Too Edgy for
    American Homes?. *Wall Street Journal*, pp. A1 & A12.

Cell Press (August 20, 2007). *Girls prefer pink, or at least a redder shade
    of blue*. Retrieved April 29, 2009, from http://wwweurekalert.org/
    pub_releases/2007-08/cp-gpp081507.php

Centre for Confidence and Well-being (n.d.). *Overview and Research*. Re-
    trieved April 24, 2009, from http://www.centreforconfidence.co.uk/
    flourishing-lives.php?p=cGlkPTE3MyZpZD02NjQ

Classic Nursery (n.d.). *Landscape Design* . Retrieved May 18, 2009, from
    http://www.classicnursery.com/investment.php

Colour Affects (n.d.). *How it Works; What exactly is colour psychology?*.
    Retrieved April 29, 2009, from http://www.colour-affects.co.uk/how-
    it-works

Cruz, H. (2008,). The Savings Game. *Tribune Media Services*. Retrieved from
    http://www.hometownvalues.net/index.php?con=moneysave&id=5

Debbie Zimmer, The Rohm and Haas Paint Quality Institute (n.d.). *Color Psychology*. Retrieved April 29, 2009, from http://www.rentaldecorating. com/color_psychology.htm

DreamHomeDecorating.com (n.d.). *Psychological Effects of the Color Orange*. Retrieved June 22, 2009, from http://www.dreamhomedecorating. com/psychological-effects-color-orange.html

Flynn, C. (n.d.). *The Psychology of Colour*. Retrieved April 29, 2009, from http://hubpages.com/hub/The-Psychology-of-Colour

HGTV (Producer)(Executive Producer). (,). [Television broadcast]. : .

HGTV (n.d.). *Design for Happiness*. Retrieved May 12, 2009, from http://www. hgtv.com/decorating/design-for-happiness/pictures/index.html

Haviland-Jones, J., Ph.D., & Wilson, P., Ph.D. (2005). Fragrance: Emotion, Sensuality and Relationships. *The Sense of Smell Institute, November*, 1-33. Retrieved from http://www.senseofsmell.org/papers/Haviland_ Emotion_Sens.pdf

Herman Miller (2008). *Home Sweet Office Comfort in the Workplace*. Retrieved May 14, 2009, from http://www.jamarshall.com/Portals/0/ HMRS%20-%20Home%20Sweet%20Office.pdf

Hotz, R. L. (2009, June 19). A Wandering Mind Heads Straight Towards Insight. *The Wall Street Journal*, p. pp. A11.

How to Estimate Costs of Kitchen Remodeling. (). *eHow Home & Garden edition*. doi: http://www.ehow.com/how_2146712_estimate-costs-kitchen-remodel.html

Human Behavior and the Interior Environment. (1997). *U.S. Army Corps of Engineers, Design Guides*, 2, 1-9. doi: http://140.194.76.129/publications/design-guides/dg1110-3-122/c-2.pdf

ING (2008). *Retirement Number Study*. Retrieved March 19, 2008, from http:// www.ing-usa.com/us/aboutING/Newsroom/pressreleases/1043610. html

Inclusive Design for Getting Outdoors (June 10, 2007). *How does the outdoor environment affect older people's quality of life?* . Retrieved April 20, 2009, from http://www.idgo.ac.uk/older_people_outdoors/outdoor_environment_qol.htm

JNK Products (n.d.). *Garage Flooring and Garage Storage Projects Increase Space by up to 25%*. Retrieved April 20, 2009, from http://www.jnkproducts.com/garage-storage-article.htm

Jennifer B (July 25, 2008). *Nature is Good for Mental and Physical health- For Students and Teachers*. Retrieved April 30, 2009, from http://www.brighthub.com/education/k-12/articles/3097.aspx

Jennifer Openshaw, Currents (March 2002). *Pulling Their Own Purse Strings*. Retrieved March 10, 2008, from http://www.3gf.org/news_currents.html

Jessica Bryan, AllExperts (July 20, 2006). *Buying or Selling a Home - How much does adding a garage increase value*. Retrieved April 20, 2009, from http://en.allexperts.com/q/Buying-Selling-Home-1476/adding-garage-increase-home.htm

John E. Williams, EzineArticles (n.d.). *Do Flowers Scents Make Good Business Sense?*. Retrieved April 30, 2009, from http://ezinearticles.com/?Do-Flowers-Scents-Make-Good-Business-Sense?&id=1105689

Joseph, A. (). Hospitals That Heal. *Asian Hospital & Healthcare Management*. Retrieved from http://www.asianhhm.com/healthcare_management/hospitals_heal.htm

Kitchen Remodel Ideas (n.d.). *A Woman's Guide to Great Kitchens*. Retrieved May 12, 2009, from http://www.kitchenremodelideas.com/cabinets/choosing-kitchen-cabinets/

Koco, L. (May 8, 2006). Women Facing Retirement Amid Uncertainty. *National Underwriter Life & Health*, (), 21.

Kostrunek, S. (2005). Find Strength in Numbers: Sell To Women 50 and Over. *National Underwriter Life & Health*, *109*(41), 16, 32.

Kovacs, J. S. (2009, March). Lose Weight While You Sleep. *Glamour Magazine*, 237-241.

Leaman, D. (). The Yin and Yang of Day and Night. *Catalyst Magazine*. Retrieved from http://www.catalystmagazine.net/component/content/article/81/709-the-yin-and-yang-of-day-and-night?tmpl=component&print=1&page=

Letterese, A. (2002). Women and Retirement Wake-Up Call!. *Motley Fool*. Retrieved from http://www.fool.com/retirement/retireeport/2000/retireeport000612.htm

MI Woolies (n.d.). *Wool- The Miracle Fibre*. Retrieved May 12, 2009, from http://www.miwoollies.com/index.cfm/Wool_Bedding

Marriage and Money. (). *Money Magazine*. doi: http://money.cnn.com/magazines/moneymag/marriage_money/

Meerow, A. W., & Black, R. J. (August 1991, August). Chapter IX. Landscaping to Conserve Energy: A Guide to Microclimate Modification. *University Of Florida, Florida Extension Service, Energy Information Document 1028*, 1-9.

Merino Inovation.Com (n.d.). *About Merino*. Retrieved May 12, 2009, from http://www.merinoinnovation.com/awi/en/Home/about+merino/Proof/proof_health_en

Merrill Lynch (2005). *MLIM Survey Finds: When It Comes to Investing, Gender a Strong Influence on Behavior*. Retrieved March 20, 2008, from http://www.ml.com/index.asp?id=7695_7696_8149_46028_47486_47543

Mesquita, G., & Reimao, R. (2007). Nightly Use of Computers on Adolescents. . Retrieved from http://www.scielo.br/pdf/anp/v65n2b/12.pdf

Millan, O., & Piskaldo, K. (1999). Men, Women and Money. *Psychology Today*, 1-6. Retrieved from http://www.psychologytoday.com/articles/index.php?term=19990101-000035&page=1

Munger, D. (2008). Flowers really do make you happy. *Cognitive Daily* .

Munger, D. (2008). Flowers really do make you happy. *Cognitive Daily*. Retrieved from http://scienceblogs.com/cognitivedaily/2008/04/flowers_really_do_make_you_hap.php

Munger, D. (2008, April 17). Flowers really do make you happy. *Science Blogs Cognitive Daily*.

National Sleep Foundation (n.d.). *How Much Sleep Do We Really Need?*. Retrieved March 21, 2009, from http://www.sleepfoundation.org/site/c.huIXKjM0IxF/b.2417325/k.3EAC/How_Much_Sleep_Do_We_Really_Need.htm

Nature reduces stress in rural children, Cornell Researchers Report. (Jul 27, 2004). *Place-Based Educational Evaluation Collaborative*. doi: http://www.peecworks.org/PEEC/PEEC_Research/S0009D4BC-0009D4BD

Nowlan, M. H. (2006, October 2). Women doctors, their ranks growing, transform medicine. *The Boston Globe*. Retrieved from http://www.boston.com/yourlife/health/diseases/articles/2006/10/02/women_doctors_their_ranks_growing_transform_medicine/

Peace With Cake (April 19, 2009). *Emotional Eating, Stress Management and Emotional Eating*. Retrieved April 20, 2009, from http://peacewithcake.com/emotional-eating-stress-management-and-playing-outside/

Regnier, P., & Gengler, A. (2006). Men, Women...and Money. *Money Magazine*. Retrieved from http://money.cnn.com/2006/03/10/pf/marriage_short_moneymag_0604/index.htm

Remodeling Cost Vs. Value Report 2008-2009. (Cost vs. Value). *Remodeling Magazine*. doi: http://www.remodeling.hw.net/2008/costvsvalue/national.aspx

Rona (n.d.). *How to prepare for your kitchen renovation project*. Retrieved April 29, 2009, from http://www.rona.ca/content/planning-kitchen_planning-guides_pointers

Sachs, A. (2006). Women and Money. *Time*. Retrieved from http://www.time.com/time/magazine/article/0,9171,1154213,00.html

Scent Effects (2008, August). *Allure*, 170.

Seigel, J. http://facweb.stvincent.edu/Academics/cepe/Articles/Siegel.html

http://www.schwab-global.com/public/schwab-gcb-en/investing_from_outside_the_us/glossary?cmsid=P-957158&lvl1=investing_from_outside_the_us&lvl2=glossary#i

Smith, A. (). Bathroom Renovation - A Good Investment?. *Do It Yourself*. Retrieved from http://www.doityourself.com/stry/bathroom-renovation

Smith, R. A. (2008, March 13). Fashion Online: Retailers Tackle the Gender Gap. *Wall Street Journal*, p. D1.

Social Security Privatization (March 21, 2005). *Retirement Needs of Baby Boomers are Different*. Retrieved My 18, 2009, from http://www.

mynippon.com/social-security-privatization/2005/03/retirement-needs-of-baby-boomers-are.html

Staff (2007, November 18). Mother Nature: Raising healthier kids. *USA Weekend*, pp.

Stearn, L. (2006, July 30). Women, Divorce and Finances. *The San Diego Union-Tribune*. Retrieved from http://www.signonsandiego.com/uniontrib/20060730/news_mz1b30women.html

Steingarten, J. (2009, March). Scents of Place. *Vogue*, 459-461, 506.

Study Shows Men Invest Differently Than Women. (2008, February). *Wealth Manager Newsletter*, .

Study Shows Men Invest Differently Than Women. (2008, February). *Wealth Management Newsletter*, 1, .

Study: Gender Influences Investing Style. (2006). *Financial Advisor Magazine*. doi: http://financialadvisormagazine.com/fa-news/2534.html

TTFWEB, TTFWEB. (2006, November 19). Kitchen Lighting Plan. Message posted to http://10kkitchenremodel.blogspot.com/2006/11/kitchen-lighting-plan.html

The CollegeBound Network (2008). *Sunlight Therapy- Natural Medicine for Natural Healing?*. Retrieved May 14, 2009, from http://www.articlesbase.com/alternative-medicine-articles/sunlight-therapy-natural-medicine-for-natural-healing-393516.html

True II, G. N. (n.d.). *Flowers Help Patients Recover*. Retrieved April 30, 2009, from http://www.articledashboard.com/Article/Flowers-help-patients-recover/817765

U.S Government Accountability Office (October 11, 2007). *Retirement Security: Women Face Challenges in Ensuring Financial Security in Retirement*. Retrieved May 18, 2009, from http://www.gao.gov/products/GAO-08-105

U.S. Army Corps of Engineers. (1997). *Design Guide for Interiors* [Brochure]. : Author.

U.S. Census 2000 (n.d.). *Married Couples by Differences in Ages Between Husbands and Wives: 1999*. Retrieved May 18, 2009, from http://www.allcountries.org/uscensus/56_married_couples_by_differences_in_ages.html

U.S. Social Security Administration (2009). *Monthly Statistical Snapshot, August 2009*. Retrieved September 19, 2009, from http://www.ssa.gov/policy/docs/quickfacts/stat_snapshot/

USAA (February 13, 2009). *Does It Pay to Renovate Your Home?*. Retrieved March 30, 2009, from https://www.usaa.com/inet/ent_utils/McStaticPages?key=advice_does_it_pay_to_renovate_home

Unhappy Ending. (2007). *People*, *68*(11). doi: http://www.people.com/people/archive/article/0,,20060247,00.html

University of Minnesota (n.d.). *Sustainable Urban Landscape Information Series Healing Gardens*. Retrieved March 22, 2009, from http://www.sustland.umn.edu/design/healinggardens.html

VanDerZanden, A. (May 1, 2006). Strategies to Maximize Your Landscape Dollar. *Iowa State University, University Extension, Extension News*. Retrieved from http://www.extension.iastate.edu/news/2006/may/070101.htm

Wall, G., & Bahr, C. (n.d.). *Why Women Need detriment Planning More than Men Do*. Retrieved May 18, 2009, from http://www.wife.org/retire-plans.htm

Weiss, R. (2007, June 5). Noise Pollution Takes Toll on Health and Happiness. *Washington Post*. Retrieved from http://www.washingtonpost.com/wp-dyn/content/article/2007/06/04/AR2007060401430.html

White Hutchinson Leisure & Learning Group (2000). *Learning from the Black Box: A Decade of Lessons*. Retrieved March 19, 2009, from http://www.whitehutchinson.com/leisure/articles/63.shtml

Williams, K. (). Women and Investing Be the Captain of Your Financial Life. *Womens Media*. Retrieved from http://www.womensmedia.com/new/Williams-Kathleen-Investing-for-Women.shtml

Women's Institute for a Secure Retirement (December 4, 2004). *Symposium: An Uphill Climb for Women: Building Retirement Income Security*. Retrieved May 19, 2009, from http://www.wiserwomen.org/portal/index.php?option=com_content&task=view&id=75&Itemid=23

Wright, A. (1997). Colour Psychology. *House & Garden U.K.*, 75- 86.

Wright, J. (April 24, 2007, April 24). Why exercise in the great outdoors is bet-

ter. *The Independent*. Retrieved from http://www.independent.co.uk/
life-style/health-and-wellbeing/health-news/why-exercise-in-the-
great-outdoors-is-better-446039.html

Yildirim, K., Akalin-Baskaya, A., & Hidayetoglu, M. L. (2006). *Effects of indoor color on mood and cognitive performance* [Abstract]. Retrieved
from http://www.sciencedirect.com/science?_ob=ArticleURL&_
udi=B6V23-4M1TSTR-2&_user=10&_rdoc=1&_fmt=&_
orig=search&_sort=d&view=c&_acct=C000050221&_version=1&_
urlVersion=0&_userid=10&md5=c203df9c7283c6f447aa7ecc6aae1
1b1.

Younique Designs (n.d.). *Colour Psychology*. Retrieved April 29, 2009, from
http://www.youniquedesigns.co.uk/Colour%20Psychology.pdf

Zweig, J.Staff (2009, May 9). For Mother's Day, Give Her Reins to the Portfolio. *Wall Street Journal*. Retrieved from http://online.wsj.com/article/
SB124181915279001967.html

• •

www.ingramcontent.com/pod-product-compliance
Lightning Source LLC
Chambersburg PA
CBHW020202200326
41521CB00005BA/222